The Job Hunter's Crystal Ball

The Job Hunter's Crystal Ball

*Read the Minds of
Employers and Influence
Their Decisions*

Stanley Wynett

ADAMS MEDIA
Avon, Massachusetts

Published by
Adams Media, an F+W Publications Company
57 Littlefield Street, Avon, MA 02322. U.S.A.
www.adamsmedia.com

ISBN: 1-59337-392-9

Printed in Canada.

J   I   H   G   F   E   D   C   B   A

Library of Congress Cataloging-in-Publication Data
Wynett, Stanley.
The job hunter's crystal ball :
read the minds of employers and influence their decisions / by Stanley Wynett.
p.   cm.
Includes index.
ISBN 1-59337-392-9
1. Job hunting. I. Title.
HF5382.7.W96 2005
650.14--dc22
2005026443

This publication is designed to provide accurate and authoritative information with
regard to the subject matter covered. It is sold with the understanding that the publisher
is not engaged in rendering legal, accounting, or other professional advice. If legal advice
or other expert assistance is required, the services of a competent professional person
should be sought.
—From a *Declaration of Principles* jointly adopted by a Committee of the
American Bar Association and a Committee of Publishers and Associations

Many of the designations used by manufacturers and sellers to distinguish their products
are claimed as trademarks. Where those designations appear in this book and Adams
Media was aware of a trademark claim, the designations have been printed with initial
capital letters.

This book is available at quantity discounts for bulk purchases.
For information, please call 1-800-872-5627.

Contents

What Makes This Book Different?

Finding a job has become an industry unto itself. Books on job-hunting abound—all of them dispensing roughly equivalent advice on how to write a resume, dress for success, and impress an interviewer. In writing *The Job Hunter's Crystal Ball*, I set out to write a specialized book that penetrates the minds of men and women who do the hiring. This book is a detailed description, as it were, of the mechanisms behind the hiring process *from the employer's side of the desk*. It explains the motives of *all* employers, their desires and, especially, their *fears*. You may not have thought that fear existed on the employer's side of the desk. Yet, as you are about to see, fear attaches itself to nearly every decision an employer makes at almost every stage of the hiring process.

In my twenty years of experience, I have helped several thousand people find jobs that were personally and professionally rewarding. I must confess that the hiring process has changed little in those decades, except, of course, in technical breakthroughs like the Internet and electronic resume-screening and recruiting. Beyond that, it's all a game. And you can learn to play better than the people who invented the game. *If you know how an employer's mind works—and can assuage his fears and doubts—you can talk your way into any job you are reasonably qualified for.* This book gives a multitude of examples of people who quickly landed jobs, oftentimes in just days, after using the line of attack described in this book.

By applying the hints, tips, and suggestions in these pages, you will improve your job-hunting ability more than you ever imagined. No competitor will know more, and few will know as much. That in and of itself will buy you some peace of mind during the grueling job-search process.

Finally, this book would be incomplete if I did not devote part of the book to a key problem faced by almost all job hunters—rejection. The turndowns will make you feel you're worthless—*if you let them*. Don't sabotage yourself. The feelings that can rise up and bring your job-hunt to a cruel stop—emotions like fear of rejection, frustration, and helplessness—can be reversed. If you're performance driven and not a quitter, if you're a fighter willing to do something strong, then the law of averages will take care of you. However, there is no law against your improving on the law of averages. And that's what this book is about to help you do.

Fraternally yours,

Stan Wynett
Flushing, NY
stanwynett@rcn.com

Acknowledgments

I wish to thank my agent Linda Konner for presenting this book to Adams Media and to Adams Media for having the gumption to publish it, particularly the frank chapter on the sensitive subject of lying. I wish to thank my editor Jill Alexander, and her assistant Kirsten Amann for the many contributions they made to the manuscript that made it more expansive, more readable, and much easier to comprehend. Finally, and above all, I wish to thank the customers of Stan Wynett Resumes for allowing me to use them as examples, and to the many executives in business, education and not-for-profit who answered our mail and phone calls to give freely of their advice and opinions.

CHAPTER 1

The Boss: Saving Face Can Be the Strongest Motivation

Someone higher up is constantly looking over their shoulders and whispering, "Your first hiring mistake may be forgiven—but let it be the last!"

I t's the big day . . . interview day. A day that has taken you dozens (or even hundreds) of resumes to reach. Maybe you're interviewing for your first job, or maybe it's a coveted position that requires years of experience in the industry, four advanced degrees, and the willingness to give up your left big toe for the privilege of working there. Presiding over the process with the utmost impartiality is THE BOSS. Hopefully, if all goes well, *your* boss. Just the title alone connotes something lofty . . . an individual with rare intellect and judgment. Yes, he's certainly going to preside over the process with fairness and equanimity. After all, he wants the best person for the job, right?

Reality check: Your interview starts when the boss says so and lasts until you bore him. Bosses are the infallible umpires. They have the power to give or withhold their consent. No appeals can be made concerning their hiring decisions. What they want is a loyal and compatible work force: employees who work hard, add to company profits, get along with one another, and stay put.

Old-fashioned job hunters look upon employers as filling a parent's role. But here's something those womb-seekers perhaps don't know about their foster parents (and, they hope, excellent providers): *Bosses hate the hiring process.* They'd almost rather be audited by the IRS than add a new face to the payroll.

For you, job-seeking is an opportunity. For them it's the unanswerable question, "Who is the best person for this job?" To which, unfortunately, there is no good answer.

The hiring process is also much more drudgery for the boss than it is for you. You need only write a resume and a cover letter. The boss must write out a neatly and methodically detailed job description . . . compress it into a two-inch-long ad . . . and slog through hundreds of drek resumes (for jobs that are widely sought after, maybe 500 to 1,000 resumes). And that's just the beginning.

They must also take (or dodge) phone calls that interrupt their work . . . endure hours of interviewing perfect strangers, all but one of whom they will never see again . . . repeat the same canned questions . . . and listen for fresh, unexpected answers. A crowd of thoughts passes through their minds—there are judgments to be made, reference checks, screening, choices, mistakes, doubts, lies, apologies, disappointments. They must also cope with their own inner feelings of hostility towards certain types of individuals and avoid asking any of the eleven questions that are illegal and could land their employer before the Equal Employment Opportunity Commission (EEOC). Would you really want to trade places with them?

If they hire you, you become a walking reflection of how good (or how awful) they are at picking people for their department. If they hire someone who turns out to be laughably incompetent, someone who doesn't know the maker of Heinz ketchup, both they and the airhead they hired become targets of office wit and sarcasm. The respect they receive from their own superiors slips a notch. Firing the employee, when things don't work out, is embarrassing, costly, and means they'll have to start all over again. Moreover, their reputation is on the line if they don't get rid of the airhead fast enough. Should they make a second hiring mistake, a possible promotion could melt away. On the other hand, their standing with their superiors rises a notch or two every time they pick someone who goes on to become a treasure to the company. The dazzling up-and-comers become reflections of their astute hiring prowess and superior judge of talent.

A General Needs Soldiers

In business as in life, no one can do it all alone. A boss's ability to recruit and hire competent staff is one of the stepping-stones to more responsibility. Why do you think that bosses so often ask you in for second and third interviews before they make the final decision? Or set up group interviews? Submit you to tests? Turn you over to the psychologists? Ask others for their feedback? Rely on specialists like executive recruiters, employment agencies, and human resources professionals? Even pore over your handwriting for clues?

Bosses do all of this because they have an insatiable need for reassurance that they are not making a mistake hiring you. This ever-present executive anxiety almost always makes the hiring process twice as long, costly, and full of lying apologies than it has any need to be—an incredible squandering of management's time and resources.

There is no totally risk-free way that bosses can use to tell in advance how well you'll work out. Peter Drucker, the legendary management consultant, says, "The only thing that requires even more time and even more work than putting people in a job is unmaking a wrong people decision." It's an all-too-common practice, Drucker says, "to put people in positions because of an absence of weakness rather than finding common people who can do uncommon things."

The best bosses can hope for is *that what you have done for others you will do for them*. For this reason, the *ideal* hire is someone who is (1) hired away from a competitor, (2) doing the same work, and (3) a rising star in the competitor's organization. Through shrinking the fear factor in a prospective employer (it never disappears completely), such people can almost always justify receiving thousands of dollars in higher starting pay because of their own job security that they are leaving behind.

The state of terror that bosses live in regarding making wrong hiring choices makes them vulnerable. Whoever promises to fulfill the boss's desires and presents the least risk of disappointment becomes *the best person for the job* (you'll run into this phrase a lot). You please bosses by convincing them they will lose neither money nor face, hiring you, but could lose both if they don't.

"My Boss Was a Total *#@*&!"

Just because you've been invited by the interviewer to "speak freely" . . . don't. One of the most common ways of ruining a promising interview is to sound off contemptuously about your previous bosses. Employers have serious doubts about prospective employees who have become embittered at a previous boss or organization, or who see their bosses as adversaries rather than colleagues.

Your former boss may have been the devil incarnate, but you're expected to feel toward bosses as the military feels toward parades—reverent and enthusiastic. Employers may punish you with a rejection if you answer the following questions too honestly:

* "What do you like/dislike about your last boss?"

* "Who was the worst boss you ever had? Why?"

No matter how much interviewers may encourage you to be candid and forthright, don't fall for it. They're just trying to see if you're a big enough sucker to let it all hang out. Be circumspect in your responses, and get off the topic as quickly as you can.

Get this: They'll also want to know "What type of manager do you prefer working with?" As if they were going to take notes on your preferences and then pick out a boss to please you! It's a trap. What they're really looking for is whether you have strong likes, dislikes, or preferences that are unrealistic and can't be fulfilled by *any* boss.

If you're asked this question, better to say something like this:

"My ideal boss appreciates initiative. He's generally courteous. When you do a good piece of work or something extra, he's quick to notice and let you know he's observing you. He explains things to his staff, and I'm able to learn a lot about accounting (data processing, advertising, medical billing, etc.) from him or her."

And let it slide. Keep your answer brief. Here's the time to portray your mean old Scrooge of a boss as a worthy and experienced teacher and you as the star student, learning, obeying, and planning for your future.

Make It Difficult for the Interviewer to Reject You

Why hand an interviewer a careless mistake when you've probably worked extremely hard just to be in the interview chair? Negative comments about your previous boss or company's policies, even if they are true, can brand you as hypersensitive or judgmental or a malcontent or a grievance collector or a whistleblower in the making. You'll sound like someone who needs *handling*.

Granted, we all want to be loved and guided, but bosses have no plans to take the place of Mom or Dad.

Thus, it's not in your best interest to say your past or present employer is unfair, disorganized, too political, or dishonest, or that he or she discriminates or has gotten into financial trouble. Interviewers may feel you'll be looking them over for trouble and finding it. Isn't it wiser to let them hear your voice echoing the victories of your career rather than its past disappointments? It is said that life cannot go on without a great deal of forgetting. Sometimes, still tongues lead to job offers.

Bosses from Hell

In a recent survey of visitors to *www.badbossology.com*, a Web site devoted to the study of bad bosses, 48 percent said they would fire their bosses if they could, and 26 percent said they would have their bosses analyzed by a psychologist. Sadder still, only 1 percent of workers surveyed feel the human resources department "is helpful in resolving their problems with a difficult boss."

Saul Gellerman, the author and motivational psychologist, once said, "Bad bosses are almost never all bad. They are usually very good in the technical aspects of their jobs, or in tasks that require specialized knowledge or skills, but rather clumsy in their motivation of workers." So why doesn't top management replace bad bosses? More often than not it's because they are too busy trying to be successful themselves. It's also a harsh reality that before a bad boss can be rehabilitated, he or she must be sold on the idea that he or she is a problem child. Who's going to do that? It takes guts to tell a boss that, and that's why most bad bosses stay in their jobs and stay bad—at least until productivity suffers or a lawsuit arises.

You and the Boss: An Unequal Relationship

What most workers envy about their bosses are their pay, perks, and ability to come and go as they please; meanwhile, they ignore a boss's responsibilities and long hours. Recognizing your boss's superior status and accepting that you are not equal, just as parents and children and teachers and students are not equal, is a factor that will help you in your working relationship.

The relationship you have with your boss is a *vertical* relationship. You don't have equal status; you don't have the same control, duties, or wages as your boss. You confer dependency on yourself when you apply for a job, and some people resent that dependence. Your boss has authority over you and can reward, punish, and control you. Your boss is the leader, and you are supposed to be the follower.

The lack of equality in this vertical relationship irritates workers, who may feel they are more competent than their bosses. But there really shouldn't be a problem. The theory is that the leader can help the follower perform the job correctly and learn skills needed to move up in the organization. The followers need only show up on time, be productive, and help the leaders to do their jobs. It's a nice theory, but it never works that way. That's why people have written enough how-to-get-along-with-your-boss books to fill a wing of the Library of Congress.

The New Boss, and the Old One

Whenever you are looking for a new job, you are also—whether you like it or not—looking for a new boss. *The Job Hunter's Crystal Ball* is designed to help you to understand things from the point of view of employers, so that you can tailor your job search to get them to decide in your favor. As you consider how to impress a new potential boss, it's a good time to investigate the relationship you have with your current one. What you can learn about how to get along (and how *not* to get along) with bosses will be of benefit to you in your job hunt and throughout your career.

Check Your Negative Attitude at the Door

Though you may try to conceal a negative attitude toward your boss, even a hidden attitude can hurt your relationship. You may find that there's just something about your boss that you dislike. Perhaps he or she awakens some secret hurt in you. Perhaps your supervisor reminds you of a teacher or a neighbor you don't like. Or maybe your boss reminds you of another supervisor you had in a previous job to whom you reacted negatively. You may want to look inside yourself for the source of the irritation and see if a past negative experience is now turning you off to your present boss.

Since your boss is the key to your success at work, see what you can do to build the boss's confidence in you and increase your promotability. This is not to suggest that you do something as shameful as working hard to "cozy up" to your boss. Adopting the following measures would be a truly generous and effective way for you to do everything you can to improve your relationship with your boss:

Grow the right attitude. You can *grow* the attitudes that win promotions, more pay, more status, and more happiness at work. There are things you might not like to do but you do all the same because you know it's the smartest thing to do—like exercising or taking out the garbage. The secret of your future is hidden in your daily routine.

Be productive. The most important thing you can do to build a harmonious relationship with your boss is be productive. Your productivity will bring satisfaction to both of you.

Show loyalty. Being loyal to your boss should require no effort on your part, but it will go a long way toward cementing your relationship. How do you show loyalty? Give your boss's ideas and suggestions a fair chance. Don't take sides against your boss. Compliment your boss for good ideas, and offer congratulations when they are successful.

Lend a hand. If your coworkers get swamped and need help, pitching in to assist shows appreciation of the predicament and helps your boss. Suppose your boss gets a rush job. You're in the middle of a task yourself and would like to finish it. Instead, you say, "What I'm doing can wait—how can I help?"

Communicate effectively. Saying things that make your point without angering people is very important in office relations. You shouldn't risk hurting people by "being honest." Neither would you support anyone who is dishonest. If someone in the office asks you to punch a time card or participate in some other act that is against office policy, you can say, "I'd feel a little funny doing that . . . how do you feel about it?"

There are many organizations that seek to wield power, influence, and control over their workers. Moreover, there are many combat-ready bosses who are mean, hurtful, and not supportive of their employees. Still, if you can carry out your program of linking arms with your boss, you certainly won't be the first one asked to walk the plank when hard times come, no matter where you work.

If You Can't Fix It, Escape

Bosses are required by those above them in the organization to get work done. Only when a boss can't deliver results does higher management consider someone a bad boss. If you're really convinced that your boss is blocking your growth and sucking the life out of you, then start looking for an escape. Don't wait until you are so miserable that you go out and accept an inferior job as a replacement. While you should seek to make your boss your ally, don't give her power over your life.

CHAPTER 2

The Screening Process: The Objective Isn't What You Think It Is

A Las Vegas hotel operator who was about to open a lavish new hotel, with over 8,000 well-paying jobs, received over 150,000 responses to a help-wanted ad. Interviewing every qualified applicant would have delayed the hotel opening until Y3K. Thus, the hotel resorted to what many employers are using in the new age of recruiting: electronic resume screening, telephone screening, and interview screening to reduce the total applicant pool to a more manageable number of prime prospects.

In such a process, many fully qualified candidates are screened out because of errors they (unknowingly) commit. That needn't happen to you once you understand the game the employer is playing and how you can alter the rules in your favor. For example, in the next section, we'll discuss how to thwart an employer from screening you out on the phone, before they've even met you.

Turn the First Phone Call to Your Advantage, Not Theirs

There is one sure way to keep from getting flustered and tongue-tied when a prospective employer phones you at home. Don't answer it. Take all messages on an answering machine (or have another family member take all your calls) whenever you have resumes in the mail. Use the phone to get information, not to give it out. The next morning, you will return the call *on a pay phone* (for reasons we'll discuss later).

A telephone interview invariably will catch you off-guard. If you're at work, the risk of being overheard is great. And if you're at home, chances are your mind is focused on yard work, preparing a meal, watching television, or maybe you got caught napping or showering. You're not prepared to discuss job responsibilities, salary expectations, or any other important aspect of a new position, especially since one wrong answer will screen you out. Suppose you're asked a question about salary (often the main purpose of the call) and you give a wrong answer. Any interest they had in you could be gone as quickly as money loaned to relatives.

Once you know the employer's identity from the answering machine, *you* are in control. If you responded to a blind box number, now you know who placed the ad, and you can reread it and tailor your response. Now you're ready to return the call, and you've gained the upper hand by being the one to place it.

Request a Meeting

First and importantly, return the call from a public pay phone. Why on a pay phone, you may be asking. The idea here is to preclude a long conversation. By calling from a pay phone, you can state that you are on your way somewhere, either to your own job or to an interview with another potential employer. The time pressure of this impending interview or job permits you to close the conversation shortly, and when it is in your best interest to do so.

Your first statement in calling back should be to thank the employer for their interest in you and immediately to ask for a face-to-face meeting. Have a date and time in mind when you call. Say, "I'm on my way to an interview/my current job. Can we meet next Thursday at 10 A.M.?"

You will be glad to know you will never make anyone angry by using this procedure. Keep in mind that they called *you* after they read your resume. Your qualifications must come close to what they are looking for, or they would not have called you. No employer likes to see a star prospect slip through their fingers when they might have been right for each other. So even if they have to wait a few days to learn all they want to about you, they'll be patient.

Dodge Salary Talk Whenever Possible

The caller may ask, "Just tell me quickly, what kind of salary did you have in mind? You didn't mention it in your cover letter." Your best response to this gambit is, "Please, let's leave that until we meet in person. We won't have a problem with salary if we're right for each other. Is a meeting next Thursday at 10 A.M. convenient for you?" Remember, you supply a date and time—don't ask them. If they again ask for salary, repeat a variation of your previous response.

Say goodbye fast. Be courteous and respectful. The objective is to hold out for a face-to-face interview. Nothing else. Don't let the conversation drag on. Above all, keep the call short, and don't try to sell yourself on the phone. Most interviewers will secretly admire your determination and your skillful use of the situation. They know that what you are doing *to* them is something you could also be doing *for* them—as long as they hire you. People are called cunning when they foresee a result and avoid the traps laid down for them.

Why Prospective Employers Interview You by Phone

In a survey of employers that my company made, 70 percent of them responded that they have interviewed job applicants over the phone. When asked why they did phone interviews, they provided the following reasons:

* "Initial screening to see if an interview is warranted."—*Director of administration*

* "As a timesaver to cut down the field to a manageable number of candidates. It also shows how well the candidate can organize his thoughts on the spot."—*Company president*

* "Using the phone is not a matter of preference, but of necessity. I need to weed candidates out."—*President, timber company*

* "We sometimes use the phone to check out borderline people to see if they meet our criteria for being interviewed."—*President, computer company*

* "Qualifying only . . . is there a reason to bring applicant in?"—*Chief executive, airline*

* "Using the phone allows me to get rid of unqualified applicants."—*Sales manager*

* "I only use the phone when I am undecided as to whether to fly the candidate to our office for a face-to-face interview."—*Operations manager*

End Your Test-Taking Anxiety

Some employers use psychological tests to help them determine your aptitude for the work, particularly for sales jobs. There is something very important you need to remember about these tests that should end any nervousness you may feel about taking them. Ready?

It isn't essential that you score high. Just avoid scoring too low. You don't have to demonstrate you are right for the job. You just have to show that you're not wrong for it. You may be thinking, "That's like telling me the way to keep from feeling miserable is to avoid anxiety." Read on, and you may find the following comforting.

Testing you costs your prospective employer time and money. The decision to test you shows that the interviewer is impressed with you and wants to go further. They just want to assure themselves there is nothing in your makeup that would make you a *wrong* choice.

A satisfactory score usually means you're in. What is satisfactory? Score close to the mean, the middle, a C. There are books in your public library on test-taking strategies. They'll tell you how to give the best possible account of yourself. Every kind of pre-employment test is analyzed for you. They show you not only which answers are correct and why, but they also explain why the other answers are incorrect. With a little practice you can pretty much project whatever image you know is wanted. With practice you can move out of the middle of the pack and up to the eightieth or ninetieth percentiles, but you don't really need to.

Preventing Interview Jitters

Clinical experiments have proved over and over that the trouble is not that people are *self*-conscious but that they are *others*-conscious. Self-conscious people indulge in continual self-analysis. After each action, they ask themselves, "I wonder if I should have done that." The real problem is that they are hypersensitive to what *others* may think of their every action.

Stop criticizing yourself. Don't be concerned about creating an effect. Many people who go to interviews act as if they were going to be put on trial for their lives. Ask yourself, What is the worst that can happen to me? You'll either get the job or not get it. If you don't get it, you'll be no worse off than you were before.

Getting Past the Hiring Person's Secretary

Let's move now to the person so often first in line to see our cover letters and take our phone calls: the boss's secretary. Secretaries seem to be posted at the gates armed with questions and statements designed to keep people like you and me out. "What is this call in reference to?" or "Do you have an appointment?" or "I'm sorry, but he's in a meeting." You can't get through to the boss, even with a police escort.

Don't waste valuable job-search time thinking up ingenious ploys to get around secretaries. When secretaries shut you off from contacting their bosses, they are carrying out the boss's wish. This is a point you shouldn't overlook. It's the boss, not the secretary, who wants you ignored. Much time is wasted by job-seekers making unwelcome follow-up calls to employers they have failed to impress on paper or face to face in an interview. A famous cartoon in *The New Yorker* magazine shows an executive talking into a phone and telling the caller, "No, Thursday's out. How about never—is never good for you?"

Don't Shoot the Messenger

Here's the right way to think about your follow-up calls to your prospective boss that are being rejected by his or her secretary. If you turn yourself into a red-hot prospect through your resume and cover letter, the employer should want to call you. They should want to send you some hopeful sign before some other employer grabs you first. If the prospective employer does not take your call, and the office now seems like a castle with a moat around it, it could be a signal that other applicants have impressed them more than you did.

With candidates they regard as good job prospects, employers dispense courtesy as an investment. Those who no longer interest them, the runners-up, are usually brushed off with a form letter of regret. If the letter seems like a long time in coming, it could be because the number-one choice has not been snared, and they want to keep you in reserve. Or it could be that the boss has made a hiring decision but is not in a hurry to send out letters to the also-rans. Or there may not be any letters. Runners-up are often badly neglected by busy employers, whose silence after an interview arouses a lot of heartache and doubt in those who didn't get the job.

One of the reasons that organizations place blind help-wanted ads (an ad without the employer's identity, only a box number) is to avoid having to reply to a ton of phone calls from hopeful job candidates who want to know if they are being considered. The ad might also direct you to respond to the human resources department rather than to your prospective boss so the HR people can perform the same screening function as a blind ad.

It's important to place a phone call after you've submitted your resume. Polite follow-up can get you in the door or augment an already positive impression. But if the person who took your resume won't take your call, that in itself is a message that you may not have impressed them sufficiently, or that they found someone stronger.

Your Case Has Been Heard

What's important to realize is that if you've made your case and not gotten the position—for whatever reason—then it's time to search out new opportunities. Don't spend your energy in rage or frustration. Adopt the attitude that you win some and lose some. If you've been losing them all, then it's time to consult a job coach who may pinpoint your problem in a session or two. Also remember that getting an interview validates your resume. You at least know that was not the cause for the turndown.

The Screening Process: Employers Speak Out

You've probably read in numerous articles and how-to-get-a-job books, by authors who regard themselves as authorities, that you should avoid sending your resume to the human resources (HR) department.

These authors contend that HR will ignore your resume because they are understaffed from downsizings. Or the HR staff will not understand your resume if you are a technician. Or HR is not aware of all openings. Or blah, blah, blah.

Of course, if you can find the name of the hiring manager, by all means send your resume and cover letter directly to that person. But what if you can't find out the name of the person doing the hiring? What if you are writing to a box number? What if the ad says send your resume ATTN: Human Resources Department?

One fact seldom mentioned is that if HR likes your resume and forwards it to the person doing the hiring along with a little yellow sticky note saying so, you've already got a formidable ally pulling for you.

To debunk the myth that HR is disinterested in your resume or unequipped to understand it, I wrote to seventy-five corporate recruiters and asked them to describe the resume-evaluation process at their organizations. Some of their responses follow here. After reading them, you should agree that human resources departments are often something more than strongholds of disinterest and uncaring.

* "Read for 15–30 seconds and sorted into (1) *Possible* and (2) *No*. Possibles are reread and strong candidates invited in for an interview."—*Corporate recruiter, large stockbroker*

* "With recent graduates, we look for education credentials, i.e., major, degree, GPA, school. Does the individual have any work experience or school course work to support the qualifications? If no, send a No-Thank-You letter. If yes, have the technical manager review the resume, and if a strong contender, interview. If not, send a 'NTY' (no thank you) letter." —*Corporate recruiter, software company*

* "Resumes are reviewed, identified for possible job matches and either called in for interview if there is an opening, or filed for six months in an active file."—*Corporate recruiter, major product testing lab*

* "(1) They are reviewed by Human Resources to see if there's a current need for the applicant. (2) If there's a need, the resume is routed to a hiring manager. (3) If there is no current need, it is filed for possible future use. (4) Resumes are kept for one year."—*Corporate recruiter, original equipment manufacturer*

* "If GPA is not shown for a recent college graduate, or if there are errors, no further consideration or response is given. If openings exist and the candidate presents his/her qualifications well, the resume is sent to our Professional Employment group for distribution to departments with hiring targets."—*Corporate recruiter, global oil company*

* "Each resume is reviewed for any appropriate positions available. Those that look like they are of interest are forwarded to departments for review. Those that are of no interest are forwarded to data entry for response." —*Corporate recruiter, electric utility*

- "Resumes are reviewed by a recruiting team, a human resources person, and a professional in the career path the person is applying for, i.e., an engineer, accountant, or computer management person. We reply by mail or set up interviews."—*Corporate recruiter, natural gas company*

- "All resumes receive a personal response. If the resume of a recent college graduate is of particular interest, it is filed by degree. If we are in an active hiring mode, and I am interested in the student, a letter and an application are sent. Applications remain active for one year from the date of receipt."—*Corporate recruiter, major chemical company*

- "Business school recruiters get up to 20 books a year from graduate schools of business with a hundred or more resumes in each. At best—at best—most of them are given a very fast scan. Very fast decisions are made as to whether to look further at a resume or not. If you leave it to the resume book to be your sales agent, you may stay in the resume book. You've got to sell yourself."—*Corporate recruiter, giant money center bank*

The above is a random sampling of seventy-five corporate recruiters, but you get the point—HR departments *do* look at your resume. Don't persuade yourself that they don't as a lame excuse for not being proactive about approaching companies that interest you. Do you want the HR department to see your resume on its own—or alongside 200 other equally qualified resumes when a position becomes available?

Electronic Resume Screening

Electronic resume screening is the new buzz in recruiting, and it is gaining in popularity all the time. Why? In short, because it lowers labor costs and speeds up the hiring process. Employers can screen out obviously unqualified job applicants more expeditiously and at far less cost than when each resume has to be humanly evaluated. This is similar to smart telephone systems that direct your call by asking you to push buttons, thus replacing a human operator. Employers call upon their software doctors to prescribe similar cost-cutting measures to the task of reviewing resumes. The following sections describe some questions and answers you should understand about these systems before sending your resume to a large organization.

How do these systems function?

Optical scanning and artificial intelligence are the technologies used. A hiring person draws up job specifications and assigns the minimum qualifications the job requires. Then he or she also adds disqualifying criteria—and turns on the machine. (See page 20 for an explanation of how electronic screening systems use keywords to search resumes and how electronic resumes are stored in a company's data banks for later retrieval.)

The machine yields its verdict—yes or no—depending on how many of the programmed job requirements each applicant's resume meets. One important thing to note about these systems is that they are completely impersonal. Resumes that survive are read thoroughly by the hiring person. Designers of the systems say they can scan thousands of resumes, rank them, and come up with the most highly qualified candidates for almost any available job opening. The finalists are then personally evaluated—by actual people, that is—and conclusions are drawn.

If the number of qualified resumes identified by the computer is too massive, the hiring person can easily reduce the number of challengers to a more manageable number by adding one or more requirements to the program. If the qualifiers are too few, the requirements can be reduced to yield a larger pool of applicants for consideration.

What happens to your cover letter?

Employers detach cover letters from resumes at the start of the screening process. Resumes that survive the electronic screening process are reunited with their cover letters later, and a human reads the two together, as was intended by their writer.

Who uses these systems?

The users of electronic resume screening processes are mainly huge organizations—businesses, universities, and government agencies—that get thousands of applications for every opening. There isn't enough time to read them all; it would take years. The Peace Corps, for example, gets over 100,000 unsolicited resumes a year and hires about 3,000 people. Andersen Consulting, the management consulting firm, gets over 150,000 resumes a year from college seniors (over 10 percent of all graduating seniors). They hire about 4,000 people a year.

After his first election in 1992, President Clinton's transition team had 4,000 jobs to fill. About 2,000 resumes a day came in for weeks from people looking for jobs with the new administration. Working in two shifts, from 7 A.M. to midnight seven days a week, fifty-five volunteers fed the resumes into a highly sophisticated computer system designed by Resumix, Inc., a leading designer of electronic resume-screening systems.

In their book, *Electronic Resume Revolution*, Joyce Lain Kennedy and Thomas J. Morrow estimated there were "hundreds" of electronic systems being used. To gain some perspective, there are 6 million businesses in the United States, over 1,200 leading colleges and universities, and 3 million nonprofit organizations. Clearly, it is only the larger employers (and only some of them) who are making use of electronic resume-screening systems.

Do these electronic systems actually hire people?
Machines don't hire anyone. The traditional interview process begins after the initial electronic screening. Then, the persuasion techniques covered in this book have the opportunity to take over.

The Shadow Work Force

Did you know that Microsoft and other big organizations have a shadow work force in their files? They have resumes on file to back up every key position. Thousands of jobs in every category are covered. These are resumes of people who may have been interviewed and approved but just did not make the cut. They include runners-up for jobs, and people whose resumes otherwise impressed the hiring managers. Their names are kept in the files in case the position comes open again—as it eventually will, in the vast majority of cases. So, the next time an interviewer says, "Sorry, we can't get together this time, but we would like to keep your resume on file," they may just mean it.

Can electronic screening hurt your chances of getting interviews?
Electronic screening can be an advantage or disadvantage, depending on what you're looking for. It's bad news for those occasions when you respond to an ad with a "reach" resume. Reach resumes are so named because the applicant

lacks one or more of an advertised job's requirements but applies anyway—it's a bit of a reach to think you will be considered.

As it happens, the computer looks only for resumes that meet exactly the criteria sought. These ever-obedient machines screen out unqualified candidates without emotion. An executive from Resumix states that some employers screen for telephone area codes. They may not wish to pay the moving expenses for a long-distance move. Or they may want applicants only from a specific region. In such cases, no matter how beautifully written your resume is, or how much valuable experience you have, you still won't make the first cut past the electronic gatekeeper if your resume doesn't meet the qualifications deemed essential for consideration.

What are the advantages of electronic screening?

Mark Gearan, the deputy director of the Clinton transition team, says, "The computer system makes it possible for someone sending in an unsolicited, unsponsored resume to get a job."

Keywords in your resume may land you an interview for some other open job with an organization, regardless of whether you're aware of that opening. This is true of most employers with electronic systems. Your resume may be kept in their databank for future job openings. Finally, electronic screening is a blessing to functional-format resumes, which many flesh-and-blood hiring people pass over on sight.

Does your current resume need an overhaul?

Assuming you've created an effective Mad Brute Resume (described in Chapter 3), you probably won't have to do a lot of work on your current resume to get it past the electronic screening process. You've already met most of the requirements of your electronic model. Keep your present resume as it is. Create a second, modified model for use when you know your resume is likely to undergo electronic screening or when you're transmitting it by fax or e-mail.

Here are a few suggestions for your electronic model:

- When you feel electronic screening may be involved, don't fold or staple your resume. Mailing it flat will better accommodate the process used to screen it.

- Type your name and address on separate lines. Make sure your name is also included on the top of the second page ("Your Name—Page 2 of 2 pages").

- Eliminate any special formatting like italics or underlining, as well as words or phrases in all capital letters (change "UNIVERSITY OF CALIFORNIA" to "University of California").

- Headings that are all in caps, such as "EMPLOYMENT" or "EDUCA-TION," are okay because they are surrounded by white space.

- Avoid graphics and text boxes, as they confuse the scanner.

- Allow adequate white space to separate sections—that is, when you finish the employment section and move on to the education section, be sure to skip at least two spaces.

- Use Helvetica or Times Roman type. They're acceptable everywhere, and available on all word processors. Use 11-point type; if you run short of space, you can use 10-point, but no smaller.

- Use white paper only. Colored paper, especially gray, is harder for an optical scanner to read.

- You may use as many pages as you choose; the optical scanner doesn't get tired the way a human reader might.

Finally, by modifying your resume to ASCII program language, you can be confident that your resume will be electronically readable everywhere. ASCII stands for "American Standard Code for Information Interchange." It's a software code that virtually all computers can understand and accept. Thus, it's easy for an employer to sift through any data bank of prospective applicants, including the many Internet commercial databases.

What does the term "keyword" mean?

Recruiting and hiring managers access resume databases by searching for specific experience and skills. They feed keywords, usually nouns, into the computer. The computer then extracts the keywords from the text in your resume. For instance, a computer scanning resumes of college seniors will almost certainly search for the term "GPA" (grade point average). A search of accounting resumes might look for terms like "BS" or "BA," "Accounting," "CPA" (certified public accountant), "IRS," "audit," "tax return," "senior/junior accountant," or "cost accounting."

What is meant by "hits"?

When a keyword in your resume matches a skill required for the prospective job, and which the computer is searching for, you have a hit. In writing up your accomplishments, work in as many keywords as you can think of to maximize your chances of hits. If you're responding to an ad, use the requirements in the ad as your keywords.

You may, of course, decide to add a few keywords to increase your opportunities for matching or even exceeding the job's requirements, since the computer ranks finalists by the number of keywords it hits—even if some keywords may not be in an ad or job description.

Which keywords create hits?

Unfortunately, there is no sure way to know what keywords the hiring person will choose. We do know that subjective, personal descriptions, such as "team player," "organized," "bottom-line oriented," "creative," "problem-solver," or "dedicated," are rarely used in keyword searches. Such words of self-praise are useless in an electronic search because virtually every job-seeker claims these traits. Thus, most employers don't choose to screen for them.

What is database storage, and how does it help you?

A database is a collection of information that is indexed, alphabetized, and kept in a format that provides easy tracking. A common telephone directory is an example of a database. A college's directory of the names and addresses of its students is a database.

Big organizations with thousands of employees maintain their own applicant-tracking databases. Employers feed into their databases any impressive resumes that survived their original screening process but that did not fit any current job openings. Such organizations may have 100,000 to 200,000 names in their personal databases.

There are many other databases where you can submit your resume. For example, there are over 1,300 commercial databases on the Internet. Applicants generally pay a fee to have their resumes entered. Organizations search through these outside databases if they cannot find a qualified candidate in their own databases (or if they don't maintain one of their own). There is no charge to employers. The database operator merely does a keyword search to find resumes that match the qualifications the hiring manager provides. You can find books and articles devoted exclusively to electronic databases for job hunters. For instance, the book *Electronic Job Search Almanac,* edited by Emily Ehrenstein, lists several hundred databases where job applicants can submit resumes.

How does electronic screening affect college campus recruiting?

Not to be outdone in the electronic-screening derby, the eight Ivy League schools maintain their own databases to help place their graduating seniors. Other leading colleges and universities have linked up to furnish similar databases of their graduating seniors. Electronic systems maintained by colleges now allow all employers to save the airfare and hotel costs of on-campus recruiting. In the past, it was chiefly the large companies that could afford extensive college-recruiting programs that reached hundreds of campuses. Now the recruiting of promising college graduates is accessible and affordable to all.

A Final Reminder

Don't get carried away or intimidated by the technology involved in recruitment. A basic logic underlies the electronic selection process. Regardless of the job, the hiring manager is looking for people with a certain set of skills. If you are familiar with the job (as you should be, even as a new applicant), you can make a reasonable guess about that skill set. When you understand this process, you can sensibly make yourself attractive to the electronic screener, and thus make electronic recruiting work for you. The more skills (read "keywords") you cram in, the more opportunities you'll have for your resume to match available positions. Your resume will become more proactive and predatory.

CHAPTER 3

The Combat-Ready "Mad Brute Resume"

The resume, usually no more than two pages in length, is where the whole job-search process begins. No employer will interview you without one. Since this document is the springboard from which you launch your job search, work towards a bona fide Mad Brute Resume, a document that shatters employers' doubts with undeniable proofs. A document so forceful and full of promise that it compels a prospective employer reading it to stop whatever else they have to do, pick up the phone, and dial your number before someone else gets to you.

After reading your Mad Brute Resume, some interviewers will be so expectant that you're the candidate of their dreams that they'll stand in their office doors when you show up, welcome you with a smile, and say, "I'm so happy to see you; can I get you something?" Many other job-seekers have told me they've already had this experience. Now you can too.

How to Make a Bad Resume Good, and a Good Resume into a Mad Brute

There is a simple way to work this magic: *with measured accomplishments*. Without "measured" accomplishments in your resume, reader interest will disappear faster than free tequila shots during spring break in Cancun. You can talk until you're blue in the face, but you still won't convince anyone of your professional value. Measured accomplishments act like caffeine in your resume. You know what caffeine does—it stimulates you and picks you up. If Starbucks sold coffee without the caffeine, it would be a much smaller chain.

You'll be read carefully when you start with *measured* accomplishments like the following—solid facts that no interviewer can put aside:

- "Renegotiated lease for over 300,000 feet of space for General Services Administration from $35 s.f. down to $25 s.f.—a savings of $1.4 million during life of lease."—*Resume of lease negotiator*

- "Started night receiving of merchandise / manpower cost savings are calculated at over $1,200 per week."—*Resume of junior accountant*

- "Retrained over 150 processing employees and cut response time by one-third / learned newly installed database in two days, then trained 200-300 others."—*Resume of training director*

- "Increased second-set of picture sales 35% by stressing half-price / although second set is always half price, customers think it's a bargain and buy."—*Resume of retail management trainee*

- "Placed in charge of recouping $300,000 in past-due bills from 300 accounts, two-thirds of which were outstanding for up to one year / made 50 phone calls a day, tracked down companies who had moved / recovered $200,000, and remainder was under 90 days old."—*Resume of banking trainee*

- "First Place, Intercollegiate Concrete Canoe Competition / organized four-person team and also pulled main oar / our canoe beat entries from 15 other schools / event was reported in the *Los Angeles Times* and *The Wall Street Journal* (front-page article)—*Resume of recent college graduate*

I could go on for a couple more pages, but I think you get the point. People who compose Mad Brute Resumes work hard to collect all the facts they need to impress and persuade. They don't fall back on overused, shopworn terms like *self-starter, profit-oriented, fast learner, people oriented, responsible for, good communicator, bottom-line-thinker,* and so forth, and then leave it to the reader to immediately impute all those desirable traits to the writer with no vestige of proof to back them up. "Just take my word for it that these terms are true of me," you, a perfect stranger, are telling a skeptical employer who needs to be convinced with facts. You may think that if you wear an achiever's hat, you acquire their achievements. Those terms, without proofs, have been discredited on resumes from wanton misuse and distortion. When you use them, you're typing with mittens on, cutting corners, and talking in a bored voice. Bye, bye, so long, thanks for thinking of us, but we prefer someone with *measured* performance. Even though those rusty terms seem absolutely essential to use for some, you are really just hitting the "Ignore" key when you put them in your own resume.

Your caffeinated resume will have no difficulty arousing interest and finding readers. Why? *Because measured accomplishments give hiring people that extra margin of safety in case their judgment in hiring you is ever questioned.* Measured accomplishments are the most conclusive evidence a boss can possibly use in defense of hiring you. You survive because of the dazzling proof your resume uses to make your case.

Remember rule number one (true forever and always): Employers pay more attention to their own safety than to anything else in the whole hiring process.

Duties Versus Accomplishments

You'll notice when you read a help-wanted ad the employer lists duties to be performed and skills required. Many resume writers feel their job is done when they write a generic cover letter saying they have performed the same duties and possess the same skills as what's advertised. That's not competitive enough. You need to go way beyond that. You need to list your accomplishments—and measure those achievements you've made while performing those duties and using those skills. Measure with dollar signs, before-and-after comparisons, percentages, numbers, and quotes from supervisors.

When you list your duties instead of your accomplishments, as most resume writers do, it's like writing a biography of Abraham Lincoln and leaving out the Emancipation Proclamation. The Mad Brute resume is made up almost wholly of accomplishments. It compels the employer to read it. Conversely, a resume which merely states duties and responsibilities is printed anesthesia because it doesn't touch the employer directly, much less aim for their hearts.

Give the employer credit for knowing the duties involved in the job advertised. For example, every restaurant owner already knows what a waiter does. They wait tables. The idea is *not* to show that you, too, know how to wait tables, and stop at that point. The idea is to show the ways you outperform other waiters—for instance, you were assigned to wait more tables than the other waiters without your drive; you contributed the biggest portion to the pooled tip money, which indicates speedy service and courtesy; you sold more wine than the rest of the waiters put together, which shows salesmanship; management received more unsolicited compliments from guests about you than about other waiters, and so forth. Got it?

It may not always be possible with every duty to convert your performance into an achievement. But it's an important area of focus that you should be aware of when you sit down to write.

Accomplishments Versus Benefits

The part resume-writers often leave out when they do present accomplishments is the part that makes the difference; namely, the *benefit* the employer derives from the accomplishment. It's the benefit that turns an accomplishment into a positive performance. Here's an example from the resume of a cost estimator.

Duty: Estimate costs of electronic warfare systems.

Duty stated as an accomplishment: Developed, with two partners, an estimate-tracking system for electronic warfare systems that validates estimates to the government.

Accomplishment plus benefit: Developed, with two partners, an estimate-tracking system to validate estimates to the government. Management was ecstatic because this resolved a longstanding problem between the company and the Department of Defense that was present when I initially took the position.

As this example shows, if you merely *describe* the tracking system your employer accepted and installed, you may leave several questions unanswered in the "show-me" reader's mind. Did the system work the way it was supposed to? Did it have unseen start-up problems you haven't disclosed? Did it require costly upgrades? If it worked at all, what benefits did it confer on the developers? There's no good reason to leave the reader in doubt. Include the benefit, and you come out with a statement that both influences and persuades. It isn't enough to get read; you must also persuade.

Use Numbers, Percentages, Dollar Signs, and Before-and-After Comparisons

When you add statistics to your accomplishments, they hold more veracity in the reader's mind and ease any fears of puffery. Words do not persuade half so well as numbers. In the business world, results are always expressed in figures, before-and-after comparisons, and dollar signs. Nothing takes their place on a business resume.

Use Accomplishments as a Unifying Theme

Major accomplishments are intended to construct a framework that will be at least momentarily dazzling. Don't digress. It weakens the impact. Relate your accomplishments strictly to the job you're after. *Big organizations demand specialists.* If you attempt to show versatility in another, unrelated area, you weaken your main theme.

Here are some things to remember in adding accomplishments to your resume.

List one accomplishment for each year of work

Employers like to see at least one accomplishment for every year of employment. If you think about it, that's really not too much to ask of a prospective employee.

Link the first accomplishment to the job you seek

As readers surf your resume, their eyes go to the first bullet under each job. If the first accomplishment impresses them, they will go on reading. When you write down your accomplishments, lead off with those accomplishments most relevant to the employer you've targeted. Link it clearly to the job you seek. Also keep in mind that your accomplishments should be things that the reader would like done for them. Even your more general accomplishments should be relevant to the reader, telling them that your skills are important to this position.

Tell what, not how

You waste precious space and bore the reader when you tell *how* you accomplished what you did. I recall a resume we helped prepare for a hotel front desk manager. The hotel was booked to capacity when a fire broke out, forcing many guests from their water-soaked rooms. Nevertheless, by nightfall, all the guests were made comfortable, and nobody checked out. Telling the story would have taken a half page of the resume, so *how* was omitted, only the result. But the writer told me that in every interview he got, the interviewer asked, "So, what did you do, and what happened?" Save *how* for the interview. When you look in the daily sports pages, you are very likely looking for final scores, the result, the outcome of an event. It's the same for resume readers. The only time you want to include the *how* is if it shows you as ingenious, creative, or resourceful. Even then, *how* might make a better anecdote for your cover letter, or for your interview.

Use your annual review as a source of resume material

Your annual performance review or evaluation describes how you function on the job, in the opinion of your superiors. This is an excellent place to find all sorts of charming compliments regarding your job performance that you can use to create a profile—such as "always exceeds expectations."

How to Present Accomplishments From the Past

It's best to include just the past ten to fifteen years of employment on your resume. If you have accomplishments that back up your job objective but that occurred a long time in the past, put them in your cover letter where no names or dates are required. This will make it easier for the reader to see you have that experience without aging you.

By now it should be clear that measured accomplishments are the pathway to an employer's heart. Measured accomplishments validate your candidacy, describing why you are the right person for the job, and establish in employers' minds they are perfectly safe in hiring you. They provide a pillar for employers to lean against if they are later ridiculed by higher-ups for their hiring decision.

Measure Your Results and Achievements

Your past performance is all employers have to guide them, and they automatically assume that what you have done for others you will do for them. Search your memory. Look in your files. Check your scrapbook. Write it all down. You may come upon abilities and accomplishments you took for granted. See if you can come up with one achievement for each year at work, whether you told your boss about it or not. Here's a list you can use to help trigger your recall:

1. What did you do in less time than it took others? (Include sales calls, typing, counting, closing deals, even waiting tables.) Everybody can be first at *something*.

2. Were you more accurate at counting or writing than others?

3. Were you always present and on time? Did you leave sick days unused? Were you always available for overtime?

4. As a supervisor, did you revise any work rules? Scheduling? Procedures? Standards? Did you cut waste and lower costs?

5. Did you cut inventory? Count it faster? Oftener? Less often?

6. Cut staff? Use temps? Cut overtime? Do more with same staff?

7. Handle customer complaints faster? Cut down returns? Cut breakage? Cut theft?

8. Can you draw up a budget? Can you stick to it? Can you come in under budget?

9. Did you sell more than others? Win prizes? Earn more profit per sale? Make more cold calls than anyone else? Revive more dormant accounts? Open new ones?

10. Did you introduce new products, lines, or services?

11. Did you simplify procedures? Discontinue useless processes?

12. Did you fire incompetent employees? Or hire star performers? Labor costs are the single biggest cost an employer has. Knowing how to manage a staff is a valuable skill.

The right way to look at all this can be summed up in four words: *more than anyone else.* You're not interested in showing anyone you're equal; you want to show them you accomplish *more* than others. You want to show potential employers that no one is better than you, and few are even as good. This is not the time to give in to insecurity. Be assured that your competitors will be trumpeting their accomplishments; you need to highlight yours as well.

Don't Tell Employers What They Are Sick of Hearing

When you're looking for a job, don't pad your resume with meaningless phrases such as "results-oriented." Instead, you should give specifics. According to a 2004 *BusinessWeek* article, the online consultant Web site *www.resumedoctor.com* looked at 160,000 resumes and found that more than half used vague statements such as those listed in the following table to describe work skills and experience.

No. of Resumes	Phrase
12.6%	Communication skills
7.2%	Team player
5.5%	Organizational skills
4.8%	Interpersonal skills
4.3%	Driven
4.2%	Detail-oriented
3.8%	Results-oriented
3.8%	Self-motivated
3.2%	Problem-solver
3.1%	Highly motivated
Total: 52.3 percent	

You should understand that these ten phrases are empty, useless, and self-defeating *only* when they are not backed up by specifics. And if they are backed up by specifics, you don't need to use the phrases in the first place. Your prospective employer is interested in mechanics, wires, wheels, cogs, and springs, not just a factory picture of a car. The employer is receiving resumes from a vast anthill of individuals. If they all say *highly motivated, problem-solver,* and *results-oriented,* it'll sound like a club with a single member.

Focus on your measured achievements. Your successes at the other places you've worked is what motivates employers to make a place for you at their table and to want you to do the same for them. You can talk until you dislocate your jaw, but the door of your future employer will remain closed to you if you ignore this first rule of resumes: *Show me measured* accomplishments.

Freshen Up Your Language

"Responsible for" is now running neck and neck with "Duties included" as the most overused, stale phrase in resume-writing. Whenever resume-writers are in a hurry or can't think of how to start, they reach for these two clichés. You can freshen up things by simply replacing those clichés with active verbs, as we've done in the resume excerpt below. Your readers will thank you for getting the lead out.

Calvin Meredith
20 Woodhull Avenue / 4D
Port Jervis, NY 10015
(516) 555-1462

Building Manager / Residential Superintendent

EMPLOYMENT
2002–Present
Building Superintendent (50 Sutton Place South) Sutton Properties Co., NYC
  • Responsible for *(**Managed**)* 96-unit doorman building, two elevators, 5 staff
  • Duties include *(**Performed**)* maintenance of public areas / monitored bill payments.
  • Responsible for *(**Verified and approved**)* tenant work requests.
  • Responsible for *(**Oversaw and documented**)* work performed by outside contractors.

See the difference? Relying on these two clichés to start every line is tiring and boring to the reader. They will be in no hurry to seek you out. Make your resume achievement-oriented and you'll outshine everyone else competing against you.

Resume Solutions for the Self-Employed

If you were advertising for an entrepreneur, this is the way your ad would likely read:

> *You'll like being your own boss and running a successful business. You don't need any special background or experience. The money you make is all yours, and the sky's the limit. You can set your own hours and ease off whenever you feel like it. You make your own decisions and don't take orders from anyone.*

Unfortunately, that is precisely the type of job applicant employers are *not* looking for. Self-employed people are generally far too independent to make subservient employees. They enjoy making decisions; they're risk-takers. That's hard to swallow for employers seeking dutiful employees. You must disguise yourself to be successful. Think of yourself as an employee rather than a business owner when you sit down to write your resume. Here's an example.

Previous:
Founder-Owner, Burke Wholesale Plumbing, New York, NY
Better:
Operations Manager, Burke Wholesale Plumbing, New York, NY

When you use the job title Operations Manager, the prospective employer is more likely to attach credibility to the achievements in your resume because you're a worker rather than an owner. With Founder-Owner as your title, who's to say whether the achievements are legitimate or exaggerated?

Just as important as what you put in your resume is what you leave out. If you state in your cover letter that you are a recent owner of a business for profit, they will want to know why you left. Wasn't it profitable? If not, then you'll be deemed a loser. If so, then you're probably too comfortable to work hard. And you may retain contempt for moderate earnings and have high-stakes ambition that no employer can meet. Often entrepreneurs come to the job market just to keep busy. They're bored. They've sold out at a big profit, or maybe a large chain bought out their lease with a big capital gain for them. These entrepreneurs who have achieved out to their fingertips have a very hard time getting a job with a corporation. That doesn't mean it can't be done—but you have to very clever about how you go about it.

CHAPTER 4

Humanize Your Resume

The average employer has a capacity for concentration that lasts for about five seconds. Reading your resume is time consuming. It's a chore that pulls them away from the already huge stack of work on their desks, and is probably the last thing they want to do with their time. If the job you're applying for is worth having, they've received numerous resumes—all with similar credentials. They don't know you from Adam, and they don't care to unless you can distinguish yourself in some way.

Making It Personal

By adding some personal touches to your resume, you show your prospective employer qualities you possess beyond those required by the job. A resume with a likable personality is more readable and can bring you results. It's your unique response to the standardized blueprint approach that organizations use to select personnel. It's a cliché but true: Companies want employees that think outside the box.

Moreover, you build a recognition factor with your reader that makes her remember you longer. One customer of our resume-writing service told us that as an interviewer showed her into his office, he remarked, "I hope you're as personable as your resume." Professional writers know that the more human interest they put into their writing, the livelier it is to read.

The Personality of the Writer Matters a Great Deal

It's extremely easy to understand the need for humanizing when you contrast a resume with a commercial sales letter, the kind that's stamped Bulk Mail.

While the sales letter seeks to persuade you to buy a product or service, you probably never think or care about the writer, because liking him isn't important. You either want the product or service, or you don't.

The resume is also very much a sales letter. Conversely, however, in this instance the *personality* of the writer matters a great deal. Your readers are at least going to have to imagine working with you every day. They'll be much more inclined to want to do so if they like you. Consequently, the humanized resume keeps silent about things that could damage you, while emphasizing your charm, personal magnetism, and your ability to fit in.

"I feel like I know you . . ."

> Readers should feel a nice, affectionate familiarity when they read your resume. You may be wondering at this point if a humanized resume comes across as undignified or unbusinesslike. On the contrary, readers like things that are different, and if you are trumpeting your accomplishments, employers will recognize your professional savvy.

As you read through the four resumes that follow, you'll find little devices that you too can use to humanize yourself on paper. Humanizing is the most effective technique you can employ to get people to remember you longer and to add color, warmth, and assertiveness to your resume.

Humanizing Craig James Ryan

After reading the following example, you may ask yourself whether employers really let you puff yourself up as the person in this resume has done. Not only will they let you, they will love you for it. Sales managers—the people to whom this resume was sent—love to meet bold, assertive applicants who are high achievers and think highly of themselves. This achievement-laden resume garnered both phone calls and job offers.

Craig James Ryan
859 Grays Lane / New Richmond, OH 45157 / (513) 555-2962

Sales–Quota-Buster and Record-Setter with National Companies in Each Job Since College

PROFILE
Q. How many times do you call on a hot prospect before you stop?
A. Depends on which one of us dies first.

EMPLOYMENT
1/02–Present   *Laboratory Consultant,* Metpath Laboratories, Nutley, NJ
(Company sells lab services to physicians and hospitals.)
- **Major quota busted in 2002:** Achieved over 400 percent of quota ($250,000) in first six months of 2002 / ranked No. 7 in new sales out of 210 sales reps nationally.
- **Record-setter:** Closed sale to one of the largest OB/GYN practices in company's history (over $215,000) during first year as sales rep.
- Won outstanding sales rep of the month (out of 20).

1/95–12/01   *District Field Manager,* Hallmark Greetings Corp., New York, NY (7/98–12/01) (Sold to independent drug stores and gift shops.)
- **Records set:** Led 20 district sales managers to 25-percent sales increase in $9 mil. territory vs. 15-percent best gain nationally.
- Managed district that led the country in opening new accounts / NJ district opened 93 new accounts in 1999 for $1,100,000 in new sales, beating out 20 other districts.
- Led district to finish third in country in 1997, with 102 percent of sales forecast.

Sales Representative (7/95–6/98)
- **Major accomplishments:** "1996 Sales Rep of the Year" (out of 13 in district)
- No. 1 in sales last half of 1996 for entire Northeast region, with 126 percent of quota (beat out 68 other reps).
- Prospected with cold-calling and closed sale with the second-largest card-and-gift store in New Jersey / a $360,000 customer, and one our company was after for years.

EDUCATION

- M.B.A., Marketing Management, Darden School, Univ. of Virginia, 1996
  GPA 3.4
  Placed first nationally in General Motors intercollegiate marketing contest.
- **BA, Psychology, University of Georgia, 1992**

SALES TRAINING

- Professional selling-skills training course, Metpath Laboratories, 2002
- New-manager training seminar, Hallmark Greetings Corp., 1998
- Professional selling-skills training course, Hallmark Greetings Corp., 1995

Humanizing Marcy Greene

If you diagnose the appeal of the following highly successful resume, you'll find two elements. The first is the novel format of presenting information in answer to a question. You can introduce questions into your resume such as those that an interested interviewer might ask. You can then present your answers as you would in an interview. The second element of this unique resume is Marcy's theme of exploiting change to create new wealth for an employer. She presents herself as a self-starter with good judgment, a team player, and a skilled sales professional.

Marcy Greene
24 Mont Blanc Drive / Mt. Lebanon, PA 15457 / 215-555-8951

EMPLOYMENT

1998–Present   ***Product Development Manager*** (2002–Present)
Burlington Industries, New York, NY
What would you like to be remembered for?
- Developed custom fabrics for Levi Strauss's Docker line of men's jeans and sportswear **/ Docker is now one of the most commercially successful programs running in America today.**

Sales Executive—Apparel Division (2000–02)
What would you like to be remembered for?
- Brought in a multimillion-yard fabric order from Liz Claiborne / brought Claiborne back to American production from offshore by showing our company was prepared to offer better service and *ideas* than anyone else.

Sales Manager—Women's Shirtings (1998–2000)
What would you like to be remembered for?
- Started this division, which was new for Burlington / brought in as new accounts many of the largest and most selective women's-wear manufacturers, e.g., Esprit, Oakhill Sportswear.

Sales Rep—Womenswear (Shirts and Blouses) (1995–1998),
Oxford Mills, Oxford, SC
What would you like to be remembered for?
- Built sales of this new division from zero to $8 mil. in first year with programs I was hired to develop.
- Brought in big new accounts like Land's End, Fruit of the Loom.

1989–95

Sales Executive (1993–95), West Point Pepperel, New York, NY
What would you like to be remembered for?
• Developed with designer Norma Kamali a black-and-color
check program and turned it into a 500,000-yards-per-season
best seller.
• Built sales in my area 10-fold – from $1 mil. to $10 mil.

Head of Yarn-Dyed Fabric Designing (1990–93)
What would you like to be remembered for?
• Was among the first to see indigo denim trend and sold it to
everybody.
• Won Cotton Textile Design Award in 1993 (out of over 100
entries).

Styling Trainee, J. P. Stevens, New York, NY (1989–90)
• Hired off-campus as a trainee and within 19 months had own
line of fabrics for the jeans trade / brought in every major
account, e.g., Levi, Haggar, Wrangler, Lee, Sears / my styling
helped build the denim division from under 1 mil. to over 5
mil. yards a year

Humanizing Grayce Hampton

Human-resources screeners covet applicants who can do what is wanted—and who fit in. This folksy-style resume has a five-line profile section. A profile is well-suited to entry-level job-seekers who may lack quantifiable achievements but would otherwise fit in.

If what you've accomplished is hard for an employer to get a handle on, build your profile on *services* you offer. Include little things like quotes and anecdotes, and recount incidents that show you at your finest. Tell your story with human interest, and you'll pique your interviewer's interest.

Grayce Hampton
675 Lexington Avenue / Newark, NJ / 201-555-2987
Switchboard Operator / Receptionist / Concierge

PROFILE
- A goof-proof and poised operator, I cultivate guests and make them want to return.
- I'm known for my cheerfulness / when I'm not working the front desk, guests ask, "Where is the lady with the great smile?" / whether I'm dealing with celebrities, politicians, or other visitors, I always try to make people feel welcome.

EXPERIENCE

2003–Present   *Concierge and Receptionist,* Shelburne Hotel, New York, NY
Most momentous accomplishment:
- During the Republican National Convention, I handled 500 extensions on 30 lines, and wrote all messages by hand. The 10-day convention went off without a hitch. The hotel's general manager thanked me and said, "In all the years you've been here, I've never seen you make a mistake."
- Answer guests' questions about New York City.
- Suggest sightseeing activities / Recommend activities
- Arrange theater and airline reservations
- Operate 500-extension switchboard
- Make hotel reservations on MAI Basic Four Computer, and type
- Greet guests warmly and ensure their stay is comfortable

1996–2002   *Reservation and Ticket Agent*
Air Jamaica / American Air / United
• Customer service, reservation, and ticket agent for major
airlines.
Front Desk Manager (1993–96)
Round Hill Hotel, Montego Bay, Jamaica, West Indies
• Assisted the Managing Director in charge of guest relations.
Switchboard Operator / Receptionist (1990–92)

EDUCATION
• **Hospitality Services of America,** Guest Service Courses, N.Y.C, 2002
• **Bochum Hotel Training School,** Bochum, Germany, 1989
• **Duff's Business College,** Business Administration, Jamaica, W.I., 1988

Humanizing Frieda Jackson

From the title of Frieda Jackson's resume, you might initially think this resume is going to be about databases and actuarial tables. No way. That's too drab. Take that approach, and the employer won't be able to get to the next resume fast enough.

Rather, Frieda emphasized the theme of *people*. How do you do that in your resume? One way is to allow the reader to hear what your previous bosses said about you in direct quotation (the exact words a person speaks). Direct quotation livens up any piece of writing and makes it sound real and believable. See the following example.

Frieda Jackson
44 Spruce Avenue / Flushing, NY 11235 / (718) 555-6924

Medical Benefits Specialist

PROFILE   • Was offered promotion, but my supervisor screamed,
                       "I will not release her under the perils of hell."

EXPERIENCE
2001–Present   *Benefits Specialist* (6/03–Present)
               Empire Blue Cross/Blue Shield of New York, New York, NY
               Major accomplishment *(to date):* Had highest rating out of 24
               specialists
               • Handle the "problem cases" referred by the State Secretary
                 of Insurance, i.e., clients who have been denied benefits.
               • Position calls for constant letter-writing to senators, con-
                 gresspersons / compose letters from scratch, with no boiler-
                 plate to guide me.

               Special Projects Leader (6/02–5/03)
               Major accomplishment: Teamed with a coworker to handle
               a very large project to shorten response time in processing
               claims.
               • Went to processing center for two months to observe errors
                 being made.
               • Retrained 150 processing employees and slashed response
                 time by one-third.

- Wrote 50-page training manual (they had none previously).
- Learned a newly installed database; among the first to be taught / mastered it in two days, then trained over 200 other employees.
- Acted as troubleshooter for any of five areas over their heads in work.
- Cleared Union 1199's backlog of 4,000–5,000 unsettled claims / came in early, worked late and on weekends, cleaned up backlog and got current.
- Earned high praise in my annual review, with this achievement singled out as basis for promotion.

Customer Service Rep (2001–5/02)
Major accomplishment: Graduated at top of 3-month training class / V.P. of customer service got so many complimentary letters about me that he asked to meet me.

12/98–11/00   *Customer Service Rep,* Blue Cross / Blue Shield of New Jersey
Major accomplishment: Uncovered $500,000 insurance fraud that had gone unnoticed by four levels of supervisors who reviewed it / was offered promotion, but my supervisor screamed, "I will not release her under the perils of hell."

EDUCATION   **BS, Computer Information Systems, George Mason University, 2001**

CHAPTER 5

Interviewing: What Makes One Person Appear Better Than All the Rest

Many qualified candidates with beautiful resumes lose out in their face-to-face interviews. An imprudent remark escapes from their lips. Or they never get over their fright. They pile mistake upon mistake until they regret having shown up that day. Or they leave money on the table because they had no formula to guide them when it came time to discuss salary. Or, in their zeal to impress the interviewer, they come across as supplicating or desperate. Applicants who are willing to do everything get to do nothing. Follow the little pointers below to make your next interview work for, rather than against, you.

You: You walk in affable, smiling, and confident for that long-sought-after interview with a person who has the power over your hiring.

Little Pointers: *In your first two minutes of exposure, they'll scan you swiftly and approvingly—or rule you out mentally. Your eye contact, smile, voice, clothing, charisma, and body language will be judged and critiqued. Each one of these is something you have complete control over. Make the most of every minute you have.*

You: "Good morning, Miss Decker, I'm Julia Cope. I've been looking forward to my interview with you. Thanks for inviting me to come in."

Little Pointers: *Greet her by name, and introduce yourself by name. Express appreciation for being one out of fifty or 100 people they chose to interview.*

Don't automatically volunteer your hand for shaking. Shaking hands is your interviewer's prerogative.

Ms. Decker: "Why were you especially looking forward to an interview with *us?*"

Little Pointers: *Act like you love the company and deep down enjoy the work you will be asked to do. Enthusiasm for the job is mother's milk to employers. If you love the work, you won't get bored and quit.*

You: "Well, the more I learned about your company, the more impressed I am. For example, your annual report said that you expect to double in size in the next three years. What in my resume most appealed to you?"

Little Pointers: *Follow up the interviewer's question with a question of your own to get the focus of the conversation back to the interviewer. The more they talk, the more information you get about what they are looking for and what their priorities are.*

Ms. Decker: "We liked the results you got with your incentive plan for the packing department. Ours has been a bottleneck. Oh, just for the record, Julia, what kind of salary are you looking for?"

Little Pointers: *The first one to mention a salary loses the upper hand, so try to postpone salary talk to the end of the interview. If you're tactful, the interviewer will usually go along with the deflection.*

You: "May we postpone money talk until we find out a little more about each other? Money is not what brought me here. The company and position did."

Little Pointers: *Except in sales, never indicate that money is your only reason for changing jobs. Opportunity for future growth is a stronger motivator.*

Ms. Decker: "Hmmm" followed by silence or one-word answers.

Little Pointers: *Don't allow yourself to be intimidated by an interviewer's silence or other shenanigans. They're just testing you—mute but watchful. You can be assured that the silence will not last over seven seconds. Break the quiet any time you wish by asking your own question. Always have a question ready to ask.*

You: "Are you satisfied with the way this job has been performed up to now? Is there something you'd like to see the next employee to do differently? Are there any jobs you'd like someone to take off your hands?"

Little Pointers: *Try to get the conversation back to job talk. Interviewers will almost always reveal more about the position than they intended if you can keep them talking.*

Ms. Decker: "First, let's talk about you. Tell me a little more about yourself. Why do you feel you're the best person for this position?"

You: "I believe this anecdote will tell you a good deal about me. It involves something my current company thought could not be accomplished, but I showed them it could be done."

Little Pointers: *A favorite question of interviewers and made to order for showing yourself off. (See the Chapter 7 section "Push Yourself to the Fore," p. 63.) Pause before you answer questions so you don't sound like you're rattling off a rehearsed response.*

Ms. Decker: "Tell me, Julia, what kind of salary figure did you have in mind?"

Little Pointers: *Salary discussion at the interview's end is a positive sign that you're considered a contender. The interviewer would not waste time needlessly if she had mentally ruled you out. Watch for this buy signal.*

At this point there are three likely endings to the job interview. Here's how you handle each of them:

Outcome #1: An Outright Job Offer

Ms. Decker: "You sound like the person we've been looking for, Julia, and we'd like to have you join us. How do you feel about us?"

Little Pointers: *Now, after they say they want you, is the proper time for you to bring up the salary and benefits you want.*

You: "Thank you very much for your offer. May I ask what type of medical plan the company offers?"

Little Pointers: *Be sure to thank them for their job offer. As a general rule, you shouldn't readily accept a job offer on the spot. The act of applying for a job automatically confers dependency status. So the strongest message you can send at this point is that you don't really need them. In order to make an employer really covet you as an applicant, it's only necessary to make yourself slightly difficult to acquire.*

You: "I really do like the opportunities for growth now that I understand the responsibilities of the job more fully. When must you have an answer from me?"

Little Pointers: *Don't be surprised if the interviewer now starts to sell you, a sure sign you've impressed them. Watch for it.*

Ms. Decker: "What is there you'd like to think about? This job has advantages that you won't find elsewhere, advantages you said you are seeking. Is there any question I haven't fully answered?"

Little Pointers: *This is your opportunity, when they show they want you, to negotiate for a higher starting salary than they have so far offered. Except for entry-level jobs, most interviewers rarely start with their best offer. Return their fire with a burst of your own.*

You: "Well, I feel if the person you hire meets or exceeds the goals you've set, this position is worth roughly (name your salary figure). If that sounds acceptable to you, I'm ready to shake hands on it right here and now."

Little Pointers: *Talk in terms of what a job with those goals and responsibilities is worth in the marketplace, not what you need or want. If they meet your number or offer a compromise figure acceptable to you, say yes. If they say they cannot go that high, ask for time to think it over.*

You: "This position as you describe it is very appealing. May I have a little time to think over your offer? When must you have an answer?

Outcome #2: An Invitation to a Second Interview

Ms. Decker: "I'd like to arrange another interview for you with our vice president of distribution, Karl Bache."

Little Pointers: *Get out your notepad and start writing the interviewer's name, along with the date and time of the interview. It will demonstrate how important you consider the opportunity. And well you should, given that 75 percent of second interviews lead to a job offer.*

You: "Can you tell me something about Mr. Bache? Is there anything special I can do to prepare myself?"

Little Pointers: *Realize that Ms. Decker's own reputation for picking talented people is on the line. She now has a personal interest in your impressing Mr. Bache favorably. She may offer you helpful insight into Mr. Bache. Be sure to ask.*

Outcome #3: "We'll Let You Know"

Ms. Decker: "We have a few more people we want to interview before we make a decision. Thank you, Julia, for coming in."

Little Pointers: *Your case has been heard. Come in style, go in style. Don't chatter on. If you sense the interview has peaked—for example, the interviewer shuffles papers or looks at her watch—you should take the initiative and get up to leave. Annoying them by trying to drag on the interview will not help your case.*

You: "And I want to thank you, Ms. Decker, for the courteous way everyone here has treated me. I know I can handle this job to your complete satisfaction if I am given the chance. I'll make you proud you hired me, and I'll never let you down."

Thinking About What You Are Worth

What do you look for when negotiating salary? You should look for all four requirements of a dream job: You like the work, the organization, your prospective boss, and the pay. However, put *opportunities for future growth* ahead of today's paycheck. Remember that you're selling years of your life to perfect strangers. They'll drain you of your youth and then tell you you're slowing down. They'll control you constantly and watch you closer than your mother ever did. But they also offer substantial rewards to peak performers.

The average *Fortune* 500 CEO now makes as much in one day as a production worker makes in a year. So, when they like you and want you, it's because you've shown them you're someone who earns their cost back doubly and triply. Don't be too timid, self-conscious, or embarrassed to politely spar over salary until they offer you what you're worth. If you don't think about your future, who else will?

Your thoughts:

* What's their budget? How high can I push them?

* What perks go with the job?

* Talking money makes me jittery.

* Can't let them think I'm just after money.

* How much do they like me? Am I number one?

* How desperate am I?

The interviewer's thoughts:

* What was her last salary?

* What alternative choices have I turned up?

* How much time do I have to fill this job?

* Do I want to go through all this again, or will this one do?

* If they say $33–36,000, they'll settle for 34.

What you're likely to get:

* *Entry level:* Pay is usually firm, as there are too many applicants.

* *Higher up:* Pay levels are increasingly flexible as your achievements are toted up.

* What's the market value of this job at like companies?

* How urgently do they need or want you? If you've made their tongues start hanging out, you can dip into their cashbox with both hands.

Sparring Over Salary

Here's how you can finagle a bigger pay package without incurring an immediate refusal or a look of horror from a determined, bargain-seeking interviewer.

First, let's consider how you can deflect a direct inquiry too early in the interview:

> **Ms. Decker:** "Before we get too far along, what kind of salary are you making now?"
>
> **Clarifying Insight:** *They want to know if you are beyond the salary they have in mind, in which case they'll cut the interview short. Usually they do this pre-interview salary screening by phone (as discussed in Chapter 2).*

> **You:** "Miss Decker, I came here looking for things other than just money. My instinct tells me you're paying the right kind of money for me, when you link pay to results. May we postpone money talk until you know a little bit more about my performance, and I learn more about the job?"
>
> **Clarifying Insight:** *Ordinarily, not always, they'll go along with you and wait. They like a job applicant who looks beyond money to the desirability of the job itself. They know that, even if the money is right, if you don't like your prospective boss, or the job itself, you won't stay.*

> **Ms. Decker:** "I have a reason for asking, although I admire your work ethic."
>
> **Clarifying Insight:** *Don't refuse their second request—give it to them. Answer the question with a salary range. If you give them an exact figure, you'll limit yourself later in the negotiation. You should reply with a range and add the tagline "... depending upon the responsibilities of the job." If you find out later in the interview process that the position will require extra duties, high stress level, weekend work, and so on, you'll want to ask for the higher end of the salary range.*

Sometimes, late in the interview, sparring begins:

> **Ms. Decker:** "You sound as if you can handle this position. What kind of salary do you have in mind?"

Clarifying Insight: *Salary discussion at the end of an interview is a sign that you're a possible contender. If they end the interview without discussing salary, it's a fair sign they have mentally ruled you out.*

You: "May I ask what salary range the company has set for this position?"

Clarifying Insight: *Try to get them to commit first. There's no harm in trying. But don't forget they are also trying not to leave money on the table by paying you more than you may have felt like asking.*

Ms. Decker: "We've budgeted $32,000 for this position."

You: "The way I assess this position's responsibilities, in relation to comparable positions, I feel it's worth $35,000 to $38,000. And I hope you will agree with me that my track record of productivity combined with my demonstrated cost-cutting skills justify the top end of that range."

Clarifying Insight: *Talk about what the job is* worth, *not what you want. Employers are not interested in meeting your needs, only their own. Use terms like "I feel" and "I believe" to show yourself as undemanding and open to compromise.*

Ms. Decker: "That's more than we had in mind to start. We might go to $35,000 with a review in six months."

Clarifying Insight: *They want you enough to bid for you. Press on.*

You: "Thank you, Miss Decker. There's a lot of money in $35,000. But I intend to earn my cost back at least triply, and make a contribution from day one. If there is any way you can increase the offer to $38,000, I'm ready to start.

Clarifying Insight: *Always express gratitude for a job offer. It's the sincerest compliment they can pay you.*

Ms. Decker: $35,000 with a review in six months is the best I can do. That's $3,000 more than your predecessor got.

Clarifying Insight: *You may be up against an inflexible budget or a solid wall of stinginess. Ask for thinking time.*

You: "May I have a little time to think this through? When must you have a decision?"

Clarifying Insight: *You've just sent them the strongest signal a job applicant can send an employer: I can get along without you. You are desirable to prospective employers proportionate to your unavailability. Don't be surprised if they now begin to sell you.*

Ms. Decker: "What is it you wish to think over? Maybe I can answer any questions you have right now. I recall you said you liked our setup."

Clarifying Insight: *If you really want the job, call Ms. Decker back the next day. If you ask for too much consideration time, they may think you went out job shopping and found out that you couldn't do any better. It's all image. Employers never want people they sense are not wanted by others.*

You: "I do like all I heard here today, and you've made a very strong case for joining you. I'll call you no later than Thursday, if that's agreeable with you? Thank you for a very enjoyable and frank interview."

Clarifying Insight: *If you sense the interview has peaked, take the initiative and rise to leave. Interviewers are used to being the person for whom one waits. Realize that applying for a job confers dependency status on a job seeker. They'll favorably notice this role reversal and display of assertiveness. As mentioned before, they'll know that what you do to them, you can later do for them.*

How to Tell If the Interviewer Likes You

The following actions by the interviewer are hopeful signs that say to job applicants, "I like you."

The interviewer . . .

* Sets up a second interview

* Brings up salary at the end

* Asks you to take tests

* Extends the length of the interview

Sometimes the interviewer will tell you directly that you are a strong candidate for the position. If so, realize that it is a buy signal, and return the compliment. Reiterate your interest and be as specific as possible. If you've researched the company and are an astute interviewee, you should pick up on and be able to talk about key strengths about the organization, such as, "I really like your company. I think it would be great to work with a team of people who have such a diversity of experience in the industry." Take their interest as an invitation to ask more specific questions about the company, the position, and the interviewer's professional experience and background.

If the interviewer likes you, he'll relax. If you like the interviewer, then you'll relax. The interviewer may give you the benefit of any doubts and empathize with you. It's a terrible chore to talk at length with someone you don't like.

However, don't become preoccupied trying to figure out whether or not the interviewer likes you. You'll know by noticing any of the above signs. If the interviewer likes you, it's no guarantee you'll be hired, but it's still nice to know you have an edge.

CHAPTER 6

Interview Etiquette and Behavior: What Employers Look For

I n addition to questions about your experience, background, accomplishments, and future salary, you'll face a number of other issues to worry about during the interview process. In this chapter, we'll tackle such topics as dressing properly for an interview, listening responsively, handling a group interview, and composing thank-you letters. Learning to anticipate what employers are hoping and looking for in all of these areas will put you several steps ahead of your competition.

Interview Dress Guide

There is one characteristic that engenders an intense emotional reaction in prospective employers: the way you look when you make your entrance. Though clothes may not make the man, they can certainly damn him. They may look you over approvingly and look forward to spending the next sixty minutes with you, or they may hiss you off the stage and cut your interview short.

Realize the Job Is Now Yours to Lose

They would not have invited you in for a face-to-face interview, from a pool of 600 resumes, if your resume and cover letter did not convince them you could perform the work to their satisfaction. You've already stirred up so much enthusiasm in them that they want to meet you. You've risen from applicant to contender. Now they want to see how you'll *fit in*. The interview is to determine if you can look and act like one of them.

First Judgments Based on Appearance Are Almost Always Wrong

But that doesn't stop people from making them. Everybody knows the very wise maxim (now more than four centuries old) that you can't judge a book by its cover. It means, of course, that when you have only seen the surface of something, you can't know what is inside; thus, you should examine and consider everything before reaching a conclusion.

However, despite those centuries of good advice, employment interviewers still do exactly the opposite: They judge the book by its cover. They involuntarily push logic aside and let their biases take over. And those biases are inexorable. But interviewers are not. They will avoid candidates who affront their dress code and choose someone else. People who dress alike are quite likely to think alike. Trivial as some grooming mistakes may seem, they irritate some people and put off others, particularly if the person hiring you will be working alongside you. Conventional morality is often more cruel than the law, and though it is pure prejudice against those who are different, conventional morality, unreasonable as it is, prevails over justice.

This Is Not the Time to Express Your True Inner Self

Here's the principle to remember when it comes to business dress: *In successful job hunting, expediency may require you to dress against your convictions without altering them.* You may be a laid-back personality who prefers casual clothes, but if your prospective employer has a culture of formal dress, you need to save T-shirts and jeans for your time away from the office.

Just Don't Look Too Obviously *Wrong* for the Organization

You don't have to dress in Paris couture, or attempt to dress in such a way as to outshine every other applicant. All that's required is that you groom yourself in a conservative way, and avoid the murderous (to your candidacy) mistakes described in the dress codes that follow. If you get the job, you may say, "O, Interview Dress Guide, I have you to thank for this." What times we live in!

Interview Dress Guide

Men

Approving glances:

- Hair neatly trimmed (the first thing they notice)
- Nails neatly manicured
- Dark or light suit (subtle pattern or stripe okay)
- Shirt: white or blue
- Tie: becoming but inconspicuous
- Socks: dark, solid color, not drooping
- Shoes well shined, no scuffs

Taking chances:

- Too-trendy suit or shirt
- Short-sleeve shirt
- White socks
- Bow tie
- Heavily tinted glasses
- Blazer or sports jacket
- Fraternity or lodge pins or rings
- Beard

Killing looks:

- Unpressed suit
- Hair below collar, rat tail, Mohawk
- Western boots, jeans
- Polished fingernails

- Earrings, ornate necklaces, bracelets

- Body piercing

- Tattoos

YUCK!

- Bitten-down fingernails

- Breath that could kill flies

- Dandruff

- Body odor

- Frayed cuffs, collar

- Chewing gum

- Smoking

Women

Approving glances:

- Hair (first thing noticed) trimmed and styled; shouldn't fall onto your face when you move

- Nails neatly manicured (no garish polish)

- Conservative business suit, or dress with a jacket, midcalf or knee-length hemline

- Shoes, pump or heel, no flats

- Complementing blouse, shoes, hose, makeup

- Blouse with conservative neckline, no cleavage

- Nylons, plain designs, light or dark (but not white)

- Briefcase and/or handbag (clutch); carry one but not both.

* Pearls
* Minimal understated jewelry

Taking chances:

* Unpressed suit or dress
* Clothes that are noticeably too loose or too tight
* Unstyled hair
* Loud plaids or floral prints; pastel shades
* Patterned stockings, designer nylons
* Man's-style tie
* Skirt or dress too tight, too short, too long
* Clothes/shoes that could be considered evening wear
* Too-trendy hairstyle or clothes
* Tattoos

FORGET IT!

* Bitten-down fingernails, excessively long nails
* Plunging neckline, skirt or dress with high slit
* Ornate jewelry, gaudy and conspicuous
* Heavy or stale perfume
* Perspiration or feminine odor
* Chewing gum
* Smoking (or smoker's breath)
* Stockings with runs
* Colored hair with roots showing

Be Quiet and Listen

Not being a good listener during an interview is a major human-relations mistake. Responsive listening takes practically no talent or brains. Being a good listener encourages your interviewer to open up to you. If you are an attentive listener, *interviewers will almost always volunteer more information about the job than they intended.* There is no limit to what you can learn by listening and asking questions. Here are a few suggestions.

Face the interviewer. Look directly at her without staring. Lean slightly toward her, so you catch every word. Tilt your chin up. Ninety percent of your communications with others is nonverbal. Nod your head up and down *gently* and approvingly at appropriate times to show them you understand or agree. Even if the interviewer doesn't consciously realize it, your willingness to listen to her makes her feel important.

Read Their Body Signals

You already have this skill, but maybe you're not using it. Or maybe you're oblivious to body signals, like someone with a masterpiece in the attic who knows nothing about art. Nonverbal communication accounts for 90 percent of human communication. Remember that. And 70 percent of that 90 percent radiates from our facial muscles. "When you smile, frown, smirk, scowl, wink, roll your eyes, nod your head slowly up and down, you're involved in the most sophisticated element in nonverbal communication," says John Molloy, an authority on body language. Molloy says a person whose arms are folded is signaling a break in communications, while an open posture indicates responsiveness to what the other person is saying. A quick way to build rapport with interviewers is to mirror their gestures. If they are sitting with their legs crossed, do the same.

Don't nod and accept *everything* interviewers say or they'll recognize at once it's just a device, not the true enthusiasm for the job. You'll add voice responses like "Uh-huh" or "I follow you" to show you are with them. Or, when probing for information, "Really? Why so?" Or, to keep the host talking, "I'm curious to know if you think oil prices will affect your profits" or "What is the situation at present? What do you think should be done?" Vary your routine, use it sparingly, and you'll look relaxed, natural, and involved. Listen for tones or inflections in the interviewer's voice.

What else can you do to show careful listening? When someone is talking, think about *what* they are saying, not how you plan to respond. Don't interrupt the speaker, and don't rush your response. If you listen and think before you speak, you'll make it clear you've thought about what you are going to say. Clarify what the interviewer tells you and repeat it, like so.

Interviewer: *I like a supervisor who looks for work well done and praises the one who did it. It motivates the employee to do even more, and costs us nothing.*
You: *I agree that praise is the lowest cost incentive.*

Try out this responsive listening approach on a stranger. See how flattered they feel about being listened to so closely—it's a show of respect. You're going to find this technique also helps to reduce interview jitters because you focus on the interviewer rather than the interview or how nervous you may be feeling.

Hiring decisions are not based solely on qualifications you list in your resume. They are based on *vibes* you project in the face-to-face interview, particularly the first two minutes of the interview. Vibes are the rays of your personality others feel from your look, the expression in your eyes, your gestures, your glances, the tone of your voice, your posture, poise, appearance, outlook on life, and inquisitiveness (read *responsiveness*): a thousand and one little things that an interviewer notices. With some planning and a little practice, you can control what vibes you project and the impression your interviewer receives. Use the strategies described in the following sections.

Your Lips Shape Your Life

It may sound obvious, but a smile is necessary in job interviews. In fact, when surveyed, interviewers have said nothing impresses them more than a candidate who smiles warmly and makes eye contact upon the first meeting. Again, it goes back to that vibe thing. Smiles convey confidence . . . charisma . . . kindness. Your smile tells people you're approachable and easy to be around. You're disarming and nonthreatening. People like you don't bring guns to work, don't embezzle money from their employers, and are never disloyal. *Practice* smiling. Maybe you've never given smiling a thought. Why not start right now? Practice smiling in front of a mirror. Practice smiling in your everyday life, and see whether people don't pay more attention to your words when you're smiling.

Attitude Adjustment

The next time you walk into a job interview feeling a little jittery, recall a joke or comic situation that always makes you laugh. You'll instantly feel more relaxed and project enthusiasm to the interviewer.

Handling Group Interviews

It's daunting to have two, three, or four interviewers come at you from all sides. Since the questions asked in a group interview are the same as those asked by a single interviewer, the way you handle the group is just as important as what you say.

The mistake almost every untutored job seeker makes is not to grab control at the start. Think of yourself as the instructor and the interviewers as your class. Or think of yourself as the president holding a news conference. They want information from you, and you want them to have it. No disagreement there. But they can't shout, interrupt, or all talk at once, can they? Who says they can't? You, the instructor, the president, that's who!

Anticipate that you will be interrupted, and have your response ready for them. Act rather than react: for instance, "I'm glad that question is being brought up, and I'll answer it just as soon as I answer the present one." Ask a question of your own to slow down the pace and gain thinking time: "I hope that answers your question, Mr. Webb. Has a lack of staff been the only challenge in your department this year?" Here are some other suggestions that will give you time to pause and reflect.

Don't worry about seeming nervous

Your questioners are not unsympathetic, even if they may seem so. They know you're in the hot seat, roasting and feeling awkward. They're edgy themselves, concerned with what the others in the room will think about the questions they ask.

Don't direct your answers to one person

Look at all the faces. Would you like an instructor to favor a single class member and never look at you?

Don't try to figure out who the decision-maker is

If you already know, don't make a play toward that person; you'll offend the others and come across as a brown-noser. If an individual is in the room, it's because the decision-maker wanted them there. Show everyone respect. Moreover, if you do end up getting the job, you don't want your peers and colleagues giving you the cold shoulder on your first day because they felt snubbed in the interview. Lastly, remember that group interviews are often done to see if you can maintain your composure. In this case, the way you present yourself and maintain your composure is often more important than how dazzling your answers are.

The Importance of Thank-You Letters

Maybe you're thinking that trying to impress an interviewer *after* the interview is moot. What's the point, you may ask. Isn't the interviewer's mind already made up at the interview's conclusion?

Two years ago, I surveyed executives for their opinions on hiring issues, including the thank-you letter. The results showed that 59 percent were still undecided about a hiring decision after an interview. And more than half (52 percent) said thank-you letters influenced their decision positively toward a candidate.

Here are sample thank-you letters for each of the three possible endings of a job interview.

Situation #1: When you're told, "We'll let you know"

Thank you, Mr. Forester:
I realize that interviews rarely end with an on-the-spot hiring decision.
Even so, I'm glad my resume impressed you sufficiently to invite me in for an interview. I know only a handful were selected to come in, and I was grateful to be included.
I like Emerson Electric Co., and I like the job. It's exactly the type of position in which I know I can excel. If you give me the chance to prove it, I'm confident that a year from now you'll congratulate yourself for hiring me.
Yours with appreciation,

Situation #2: When you've been invited back for a second interview

When an interviewer recommends you to someone else for a second interview, that interviewer's own reputation for picking worthy candidates is now on the line in your behalf. That gesture, in and of itself, rates an expression of appreciation, such as the following:

> *Thank you, Mr. Forester, for receiving me so graciously Thursday morning.*
> *I particularly appreciated your efforts to arrange a second interview for me with Ms. Cappel. The information you gave me regarding her department's goals and problems was just what I needed to be fully informed and prepared. You won't regret having referred me. I can make an immediate contribution, thanks to you.*

> *With gratitude,*

Situation #3: You've been offered the job but need time to mull it over

> *Thank you, Mr. Forester:*
> *I enjoyed our meeting Thursday. You made me feel very welcome, and I am thrilled you extended an offer with your organization. I appreciate your giving me the time to study your offer and to discuss it with my family. I realize the ball is now in my court, and I will phone you with my answer within the next 48 hours.*
> *With gratitude,*

As the rules of good manners have become less formal today, a thank-you letter may be something completely new to you. Consider it an investment, if you care to, but the thank-you letter is merely a basic courtesy. You want to be courteous as a matter of good form. Beyond that, you are thanking the interviewers for the extremely valuable information they gave you; namely, they validated that your resume and cover letter are successes. Those documents persuaded this employer that you are someone worth talking to. And that's good to know—that all the hard work you put into writing hit the mark as intended.

CHAPTER 7

You *Want* to Be Interrogated: Questions You Will Be Asked

Y ou'll very likely be asked one of the following questions in your job interviews. More than likely, you'll be asked several of them. As counterintuitive as it sounds, you should hope they ask you all of them; you *want* to be interrogated. Good responses can lead to praise and kind words from your interviewer—and a job offer.

The following are generally the most often-asked questions because they cannot be evaded with yes-or-no answers, and they go straight to the heart of the qualifications you are being interviewed for. Like all of your responses, your replies to these questions should be practiced in advance and not left to whim—because your answers permit you to show off all sorts of things (including stupidity).

There is no restriction on the number of words you may use to answer a question, but here is a reliable rule of thumb to keep you from being long-winded. Confine your answer to what you can say in about one minute. How much is that? Well, the average adult speaks at about 150 to 180 words a minute, and the average page of double-spaced type has about 250 or so words. So your answer could include most of the words on a full page of type. As a further demonstration, realize that from the start of the previous paragraph ("The following are . . .") to the end of this one is a total of about 190 words.

Push Yourself to the Fore

When interviewers ask you, "Tell me about yourself," do you think it's because they want to know the most trifling details of your personal life? Hardly. They want you to speak about your measured accomplishments in the workplace, especially if it's in the realm of the job you're applying for. In this instance, wax poetic about your accomplishments, and they won't be bored. Each measured accomplishment you take credit for is like a little insurance policy to the interviewer. Here are some other questions you may be asked in your job interviews.

Question #1: Why do you want to work for us?

If you are not asked this question (though you likely will be), you may want to take the initiative and, at the end of the interview, use the statements below to ask for the job. If this is truly the job you want, with a company you'd like to work for, then these are probably your reasons, and you can end the interview on a strong note.

1. I like the work:

   * It's what I've been looking for.

   * It gives me lots of room for personal growth.

   * It allows me to use my skills.

   * It provides opportunities for promotion.

2. I like the salary and benefits.

3. I like the people I will be working with:

   * They seem enthusiastic/dynamic/intelligent.

   * You (the boss) are someone I feel I can look up to and learn from.

4. I like the organization:

   * The employees are well treated, and they reflect it in their attitudes.

   * The standards are ethical.

   * Your company has great products/excellent customer service.

   * You have a good profile in the industry.

The point to remember here is that employers don't need to know that your tongue is hanging out for a job, or that you would take *any* job just to get on a payroll. That scares them. If that is a part of your present thinking, then it's something interviewers must not see or know about. It makes you far more expendable when, at the end of interview process, they must choose among two or three finalists. In *that* discussion, *enthusiasm for the job* will likely govern. What they want to hear you say is that you are genuinely enthusiastic about their company, their job, and the pay, and that you're raring to start. No qualms. No second thoughts. Not the tiniest, vanishing doubt about your desire to join their ranks.

Question #2: "Do you have experience with (computers, QuickBooks, etc.)?

"I have worked with word processors, copiers, and electronic typewriters. I have no fear of computers. I learn procedures quickly because I have a good memory. I seldom have to be told something twice. My supervisor told me I learned the word processor in half the time it took my peers. There will be no risks. I have nothing to unlearn. I really think I can be useful to you very quickly in your data-processing operations. Please, give me the chance to prove it."

NOTE: The rule here is simple: Try not to say "no" or "none" when you are asked about a qualification you lack. The "no" will stick in the interviewer's mind and be remembered. If the skill you lack is critical to the job, you won't be hired anyway. If it isn't, your enthusiasm for the job and your other virtues may carry you. An employer beset by a specific problem may value your ability to solve that immediate problem over everything else, and may ignore another requirement where you may be deficient.

Question #3: "How long would you stay with us?

"My intention is long term. But people, like organizations, go through changes and growth. I will certainly be here as long as I believe Jaspon Sportswear is thriving and growing, and as long as I believe I am thriving and growing."

NOTE: Have you noticed how often the people in power seek reassurances of loyalty and faithfulness? Your experience and skills on your resume have already been taken into account. They have already accepted that you can do the work to their satisfaction, or you wouldn't have been invited in for a face-to-face interview.

*Question #4: "Why do you feel you are the best person for this job?"
or "In what way do you think you can contribute to the success of
our company?"*

"I like Toyota as a company, and I would take great pride in your products. Apart from personal job strengths I've already detailed on my resume, for example, lowering labor costs, speeding up processes, minimizing waste, there is one more thing—pride in working for you. I can't think of a more desirable asset than having an employee who is filled with pride to work here. I think anybody who believes in a company can almost always represent its interests in a convincing way to customers, suppliers, and others the company does business with."

Question #5: "What if your company gives you a counteroffer?"

"I did not make this decision to seek a new position overnight. And I am not out job shopping. I thought long and carefully about my next step, and I've decided my present employment cannot provide it. I believe I have found it in this position. If we both decide we are right for each other, I am prepared to say yes at the conclusion of our talks."

NOTE: Interviewers are grown-up adults and realists. They know they won't land every applicant. This is just another pledge of reassurance that you really want to join them, and that you're not using them as a wedge to pry money out of your present employer.

*Question #6: "What's more important to you: making money or
having satisfying work?"*

"Are they mutually exclusive? High achievers who go on to make big money almost always love their work. Not liking the work you do usually keeps you from making it big—financially and otherwise."

Question #7: "Why do you wish to change jobs?"

"I don't want to change jobs, only environments. I like the work I do, but it no longer challenges me as it did two years ago. I'm looking for a bigger challenge, and it seems like your company can provide it."

NOTE: Here are three reasons you are *not* going to give for why you want to change jobs: 1) A personality conflict with your boss or fellow workers; 2) Dull, tiresome work, or too much work; 3) Low pay, or too few benefits. If you cite any of these reasons for wanting to jump ship, you risk having the interviewer feel

1) You may be hard to get along with; 2) You're too easily bored; 3) You're too money conscious. You value money more than pride in a job, and they value pride more than money. It's all a game they invented. You want to come off as a doer who is looking for more to do, with the money incidental.

Question #8: "Why have you had so many jobs in six years?"

"I've always been employable. In each of those jobs, I was already trained for it and got right into it. In each case, I outperformed the person who had the job before me. This is not my opinion; it's a statement of fact, which you can verify. I know this may sound corny, but I guess I just wasn't sure what I wanted. And I was too naive to realize I was letting my employers down and making myself look like a grasshopper. I know now what I am after, and I hope you will give me the chance to prove it."

NOTE: A history of job-hopping is anathema to an employer who wants someone who can stay put. Too many jobs can get you screened out. Whatever you do, *don't volunteer why you left previous jobs.* Many others besides you have been in this fix. You may have to knock on many more doors. But it's important you realize this fact of job-seeking. If you're sending out resumes and getting *no* responses, this might very well be the problem. Don't list more than ten years employment. That might help you narrow it down. Combining jobs also helps; see, for example, the resume of Grayce Hampton (page 39) where she combined three positions as reservation and ticket agent for three airlines.

Question #9: "Why were you out of work for thirteen months?"

Most of the questions you will be asked will allow you to segue into how superior you are. This one doesn't. The unemployed think first of this question when they are called for an interview, and it makes them nervous. Why were you out of work so long? What can I say? How will it look?

After you have been out of work for a long time, you'll take any job. But the prospective boss wants someone who is climbing the corporate ladder without long interruptions, someone who perhaps is younger, or who has fewer family responsibilities. Your expectations may be low, and expectations control attitude. A few turndowns and your morale crumbles, your self-esteem shatters. Nothing in your experience has prepared you for prolonged unemployment without an end in view. So you take no for a final answer and withdraw from the workforce, like a person who falls into a river and is content to sink all the way to the bottom.

There are an estimated 3 million workers in America who are too discouraged to look for work. That is something I hope will not happen to any reader of this chapter. Author John Steinbeck wrote, in *Of Mice and Men*, "I can see where a drowning man would go down, but I can't see why he would want to stay down."

Any lapses in your work history must be accounted for, that's true. Some applicants resort to the functional resume as opposed to the chronological to mask periods of unemployment. By not listing past jobs in order, they hope to keep the focus on the job rather than the time away from it. Please see Chapter 11, titled "Overcoming the Big No." There is always something out there if you adjust your sights. Why should you consign yourself to a life of bread and water when there are good dinners right in view?

Nowadays, so many millions of Americans have been laid off through no fault of their own that hiring managers are no longer shocked that someone can be out of work for a year or longer.

Here's what a middle-aged, long-time-unemployed customer of our resume service—let's call him Nick—did to get a job as a warehouse manager. Nick had a friend named George who owned an aircraft-parts business. They supplied parts to airlines the way auto-parts dealers supply auto dealers. George agreed to be listed as Nick's employer for the period of time he had been out of work, about three years. Nick gave George a copy of his resume for reference when the director of the human resources department of his prospective employer called. When the HRD director called George for a reference on Nick, George was effusive in his praise. That did it. The HRD director called Nick and offered him the job. Two years later, Nick was still on the job, managing twenty-two union workers, and had gotten a raise. Things that you might never contemplate doing to get a job when you are employed and successful may become necessary when you no longer are. Get the job. Do it on sheer merit if possible, but in any case get the job.

Question #10: "Do you think grades should be considered by employers?"

"Yes and no. Students certainly ought to have a 3.0 or better in their major. If they don't, an employer would have to wonder about their commitment. On the other hand, more students are juggling multiple priorities such as part-time jobs, substantial student loans, and activities while pursuing a degree. While those may take time away from the books, they often provide valuable life experience and skills that can be transferred into a job."

Question #11: "What do you know about us?"

"My research turned up all sorts of things about you: your products, your customer base, your advertising agency, your sales and earnings, who your competitors are, where your offices and plants are located, and a few of your achievements. For example, [relate one or two or more facts about them]."

NOTE: What's important here is that you avoid saying, "Nothing." It's insulting to the employer that you care so little about them. Most managers who have been around an organization for a while develop a fondness for it, a sort of reverence. They think about it on their days off. It's their sweetheart.

So it becomes you to think about their sweetheart also, if this is a job you want. Besides, it's easy to become good at researching companies fast. With large, publicly owned companies you can get most of what you need from public records and company statements and Web sites.

Question #12: "How would your friends (your professors, colleagues, present employer) describe you?"

There are a lot of adjectives you could use: resourceful, quiet, skeptical, thorough. But lazy, quitter, and complainer are not among them. Follow up whatever attributes you mention by saying, "If you ask around among people who know me well, I will be surprised if you don't find more or less general agreement on the traits I've mentioned."

Question #13: "Don't you think you're overqualified for this position?"

Next to having too many jobs, being overqualified is the biggest reason employers give for throwing out resumes. When surveyed, 30 percent of employers said they like to hire people who are overqualified for an open position. Of the remaining 70 percent, you'd be amazed at the things you can do to change their skepticism.

Employers like job applicants who are moving up. Seeking out a position that is a step back makes them suspicious. They wonder why you are available so cheaply and why others haven't snapped you up. They will also worry about the cost of insurance, pensions, and so on that comes with hiring someone more experienced. Fourth, they will question whether you can work under the supervision of a person younger than yourself. Fifth, if you know more about the job/industry than others at the job level you're interviewing for, you could become easily bored and quit, or you might try to steal the job on next rung up, which could belong to the person interviewing you!

The key to getting past these not-unreasonable objections is to reassure the interviewer that everyone stands to gain: the interviewer, fellow employees, profits, and you. Because of your depth of experience, you can probably take over the position right now with little added training. He'll run no risks hiring you. If you left in two weeks, the company would have more money in the cashbox for having hired you.

Further Steps You Can Take

When seasoned job-seekers swing into action, they know how to demonstrate enthusiasm for the position. They also know how to leave things out to make themselves seem right for the job. If a degree or an advanced degree makes them seem overly bright for a mundane job, they hide it like treasure. If too many jobs on their resume is the problem, they condense a few and leave others out.

If you have to, understate your previous pay and achievements. Leave out any achievement that would make you glaringly overqualified with your prospective boss. If you supervised 120 workers, and the prospective position calls for you to supervise six, don't mention those bigger numbers. Rather than omit from your resume the year you graduated from college, which omission is a giveaway to resume readers that you are defensive about your age, omit education completely. It's only important for your first job. Prospective employers will rarely if ever notice the absence.

Make yourself seem as little overqualified as your eraser and intuition make possible. Cite just enough of your background and your achievements to get you past your competitors for the job and—stop!

Finally, realize there are a lot of employers out there: 6 million. And, judging by the results of a survey of employers, close to 2 million of those don't object to someone who is overqualified. To them, you're a bargain they find hard to pass up. Maybe the job has a history of high turnover, and they're pleased to have someone of your competence in it. Keep sending out resumes, and these opportunities will turn up for you. Success lies all about you if you just keep up your mailing and networking. You can't see it because most jobs are hidden from the general public. But your mailings will uncover them, and the law of averages will take care of you.

Why Some Employers Frown on Overqualified Applicants

"Won't stay long, or they may have a problem nobody is telling you about."

—*Business owner*

"1. They will become bored if not challenged and perform poorly. 2. They probably will not stay very long if an offer better matched to their talent comes along."

—*Vice president, textile company*

"They will leave as soon as they find what they are really looking for."

—*Group vice president, food manufacturer*

"It's often a lack of self-confidence in the prospective boss. They don't want an overqualified person threatening their job."

—*President, manufacturing company*

Questions You Don't Have to Answer

Under the provisions of the Equal Employment Opportunity Act, the questions below are not job-related and can be construed as discriminatory in a pre-employment interview.

The problem is that many employers go on asking them anyway out of habit or ignorance of the law. Ordinarily, well-trained, highly qualified interviewers at large companies know the law and won't ask you such questions. Oftentimes it's small employers, who lack legal counsel and full-time HR staff (and who are also the biggest source of jobs), who are ignorant and who may ask the following illegal questions:

- "What languages are spoken in your home?"

- "Where were you born?"

- "Are you single, married, divorced, separated?"

* "Do you plan to have more children?"

* "Please give names and ages of your children."

* "What is your military background?"

* "Which of the following diseases have you been treated for?"

* "Please list all clubs, associations, organizations, and societies to which you belong."

* "Have you ever been arrested?"

* "Do you own or rent your home?"

What do you do if an interviewer asks you an illegal question? Well, you could reply, "Is this question relevant to my qualifications for the open position?" Or you could ask, "Is that question permitted by law?" Realistically, either answer will probably offend your interviewer. They won't like getting caught asking illegal questions or having their ignorance exposed. In their minds, you may be disqualified because you've embarrassed them and made them look like an amateur.

A New Trend in Hiring:
Don't Bother Applying if You Smoke

A growing number of organizations are moving to eliminate smokers from their employ. Some require job applicants to undergo nicotine testing, or they ask direct questions in job interviews regarding smoking. Does this invade your right to privacy? Of course it does. Smokers should know that twenty-four states prohibit employers from discriminating against smokers ("smokers' rights laws"). Just how bad is it for smokers? Jay Whitehead, publisher of *HRO Today*, a magazine for human resources directors, says, "There is discrimination at many companies—and maybe even most companies—against people who smoke." If you don't like being a victim, you can go to court. However, if you want the job, you'll more than likely have to go along with this illegal employment policy and smoke on your own time.

You make a stand on principle, the interviewer apologizes, but where does it get you? Probably the best course—or at least the most practical course—is to answer the question if you like the open position and really want it. You can't win these types of battles. Is the law toothless then? Not at all. Most employers do obey the law. And that's something. Realize that most interviewers at the smaller companies have no background in interviewing, much less the law, so their asking an illegal question is usually out of ignorance. In the end, you need to decide what your comfort level is with answering, or not answering, the question.

CHAPTER 8

The Best Ways to Find Where the Jobs Are

There are four ways to find a job: 1) Answering classified help-wanted ads; 2) Networking; 3) The hidden job market; and 4) Marry the boss's son or daughter (only kidding). Below are some tips for the first three approaches.

The Help-Wanted Section

Most job-seekers turn to the help-wanted section first. You may think that the best place to find a job is through posted job listings—whether they are found in a printed publication, an online job board, or a company's Web site. Almost everyone does. The reality is, while searching through such sources is the easiest way to find job *openings*, it's not the easiest way to get hired.

First, only about 13 percent of available jobs are ever advertised. Second, everyone in the city sees those ads, thus you wind up competing with everyone. It's not at all uncommon for a highly desirable job to receive 500 to 1,000 resumes or even more in response to an advertisement. As a human resources manager from a nonprofit organization recently commented, "We advertised an open accounting position and expected to get about 100 responses; we got 600." With those kinds of numbers, there are bound to be at least a couple of people (or lots more) as good as or better than you. That doesn't mean you won't get the job—it's just the most competitive way to go about it. So where else can you look?

Networking

There is no shame in asking someone for a job or for help in locating a job. Don't let your pride hold you back from making precious contacts. Contrary to what you might think, most people *like* to give job seekers a helpful leg up whenever they can.

One customer of our resume-writing service had been trying every way possible (except networking) to get an interview with a particular company. His boss at the time, who liked him, said, "Let me make one call." He contacted a friend at the target company. The interview was granted that same afternoon, and he became one of two contenders for an open position. He couldn't have done it without networking, even though he was more than qualified for the position. Carl R. Boll, in his excellent book *Executive Jobs Unlimited,* said, "I have found networking the most positive, the most effective, the most time-saving, and the most reasonable way to get people placed; do not be persuaded otherwise."

Most colleges print directories that list alumni who have volunteered to make themselves available to students seeking employment in their field. The intention of these directories is wholly for networking help. Alumni are listed by their occupations, current addresses, and phone numbers. Check with your alma mater to see if it has such a resource.

The Hidden Job Market

Some jobs are not advertised, thus the name *hidden* job market. There are *always* openings in the hidden job market. The lazy or uninformed person's approach to finding a job is to check the classified ads in their daily newspapers. If no openings are advertised, they wait and check again tomorrow . . . and the next day. When you realize that only 12 to 15 percent of job openings are ever advertised, searching the ads is the slowest possible way to look for a job. The hidden job market represents 80 percent of all job openings. Ordinarily, these jobs are filled through employment agencies, executive recruiters, friends of present employees, or simply by someone who finds the job before anyone else does.

Why Employers Like the Hidden Job Market

The nice thing about the hidden job market, from the employer's point of view, is that it solves their vacancy problem without any real effort or expense on their part. They don't have to spend for an ad. They also don't have to go through grueling interviews with perfect strangers. There are several ways you can penetrate the hidden job market.

Send out ten to twenty-five copies of your resume to organizations that interest you, *every week*, along with a bold, personalized cover letter. You announce your availability for a particular job as well as your accomplishments that make you worthy of it.

There Are Always Job Openings

Of the organizations you mail to, a certain percentage of them will almost always have job openings. Even in recessionary times, companies do hire for open positions. If your letter and resume show that you fit the qualifications the employer has in mind for an open position, you will be asked in for an interview. It's not unlikely that you will be one of two or three candidates in consideration for a job, if you reach the employer before an ad is placed. Remember, you're trying to get to them before they post the job to the outside world. Or, if your resume impresses mightily, it will very likely be kept on file for review when an opening occurs.

A client of ours was seeking an editorial assistant's job, and he was invited in for an interview after he made his first mailing. He found out at the interview that the employer had just received two weeks' notice from an editorial assistant the same day they received our client's letter. He was the first person interviewed—and the last. The employer knew Joe could do the job, and they wanted to spare themselves the expense of placing an ad and going through the long, arduous interview process. So they offered the job to our client without interviewing other candidates.

In the hidden job market, success is mainly a matter of timing and of quantity of letters mailed. If you send out enough letters, you are bound to hit an employer when 1) someone has just turned in their notice; 2) the organization is planning an expansion and will need more staff; 3) someone is about to be promoted and a replacement is sought; or 4) when a replacement is needed for someone who is to be terminated but has not yet been told. These jobs-in-the-making are known only to a few insiders.

How to Research and Conduct a Mailing

Find the name of the person in charge of the department you're interested in, and mail your letter directly to that person. For organizations of fewer than 200 employees, send your letter directly to the president. Presidents know what's going on throughout the company, and if you impress them with your letter, they're in a position to recommend you for any position.

If the organization is very big, find the name of the vice president, director, or manager in charge of the department you wish to join. Or send your letter directly to the human resources department. Most of this information is available at the public library, on a company's Web site, or by calling the company directly. Publicly traded companies can be researched in great depth on the Web.

What Do You Know About Us? Plenty!

The information that you dig up in the library comes in handy when you are asked, "What do you know about us?" in an interview. By harnessing the resources of the Web, it's possible to conduct a job search without ever leaving the comfort of your home, at least until you are heading for the interview.

It's All About the Numbers

Numbers are your friend in competitive job-hunting—assuming, of course, that your writing in the letter and resume you send is sound and compelling and has no knockout factors. With a strong performance-driven resume, you should get about six to ten interviews for every 100 resumes and cover letters you mail—if you're merely competent. If you're exceptional, four to ten responses for every twenty-five mailings is not rare. Bear in mind that these numbers are averages. Your results all depend on how good a story you spin in your cover letter and how much your job specialty is in demand.

Resist the Dump-It-All-Now Approach

Send out ten to twenty-five letters a week, rather than 100 to 2,500 in one "dump" mailing. This way, if your letter and resume are not bringing responses, you can make changes without great printing and postage expense. We know of people who dumped 250 or more letters and resumes in the mail hoping for a big, fast response but who were disappointed by minimal results. They wished they could take back that letter and resume and replace it with a new, more compelling model.

Beware of job-assistance mail-order firms who run big ads in newspapers urging you to mail thousands of letters and resumes to lists they provide. Don't fall for it. If you have to send out thousands of resumes to get only a couple of interviews, something is wrong. Your paperwork is just not strong enough, and you've paid a lot of money to find that out. Better to tweak and edit your letter weekly, if the response is not up to your expectations. If you follow the writing suggestions in this book, you'll do okay.

You can change your resume and cover letter as often as you change your underwear. In fact, if you are applying for different types of positions, you should write different resumes that focus less or more on specific credentials relevant to the job. Realize that mailing to the hidden job market is a game of numbers. You know there are jobs out there. You just don't know where they are. So if you keep up your campaign of weekly mailings, you're bound to uncover an open place at some employer's table. Here are two examples of people who did not wait for ads to appear; they probed the hidden job market.

Resume Success Story: Finding Jobs Before They're Advertised

When Gloria Hitchcock initially came to our agency, she had already spent twelve weeks answering ads in the *New York Times* in hopes of landing a new executive secretarial position. With such advertisements often garnering 200 to 1,000 resumes, such an approach was about as productive as direct mail. Gloria went three months without wages when she could have easily been on somebody's payroll—had she taken a different approach.

We rewrote her resume and gave her a list of the twenty-five biggest corporations in New York City. Each of these companies had 200,000 employees, and we estimated that among them, there were (conservatively) at least fifty to 100 executives who rated a secretary. Secretarial positions usually have high turnover. One of these executives was probably already in need of a secretary, or would be in the near future.

Gloria sent her new resume to just ten companies on the list, addressed to the human resources director. Six of those companies responded and two weeks later Gloria had a new position with a large cable network.

Gloria Hitchcock
2613 Radcliffe Road
Windsor, CT 22137 · (203) 555-0010
e-mail: hitchcock@abc.com

PROFILE   **I'll do my best, but then I always do.**

EMPLOYMENT

2001–2003   *Executive Secretary*
               Macmillan, Inc. (book publisher), New York, NY
               • On own initiative: Obtained raw data from computer and
                 turned into monthly sales reports on several hundred books
                 and authors and set up record-keeping system.
               • On own initiative: Cleaned out 10 4-drawer filing cabinets so
                 tightly crammed with files they were inaccessible—in spare
                 time / typed new folders and made files accessible in a tenth
                 of the time.
               • Learned technicalities of contracts, rights, and royalties and
                 patiently explained them by phone to authors and agents, free-
                 ing my boss to go on to other tasks.
               • Came from temp agency for one-week assignment / hired per-
                 manently after one week.

1996–2001   *Executive Secretary to V.P. National Sales* **(food division)**
               Nabisco, Inc., New York, NY
               • Arranged 15-20 sales conferences a year, plus a dozen trade
                 shows.
               • Ordered meeting spaces, rooms, travel arrangements, lun-
                 cheons and dinners; paired and matched 24 district sales
                 managers who shared rooms; organized golf, fishing, etc., for
                 recreation periods.
               • Typed speeches, presentations, correspondence, and sales
                 reports.

1991–96   *Secretary—Corporate Personnel* (1995–96)
               CBS, Inc., New York, NY
               • Learned all of CBS's personnel and benefits policies, leaves
                 of absence, terminations, etc., then answered questions from
                 managers at all levels.
               • Worked many weekends making annual salary changes for
                 hundreds of staff members.

Administrative Assistant (1991–95)
  • Typed 10- to 20-page union contracts with perfect accuracy /
    15 letters a day / updated files / prepared all sorts of reports.

SKILLS   Type 70 wpm / PC-XT / Word / Harvard Graphics

EDUCATION
  • Word Processing Course, Borough of Manhattan Community College
  • Introduction to Computers, CBS, Inc., New York City
  • Basic Business Writing, CBS, Inc., New York City

The Moral of the Story . . .

KEEP UP YOUR MOMENTUM! Nothing is more important here than constancy of purpose. Do not relax your efforts until your job search leads to a successful outcome. Now that you've begun your job-search campaign, don't slack off just because you start getting results. Realize that you don't get the job simply as a result of being interviewed and told they liked you. You have the job only when you and your interviewer agree on all terms and conditions of the job, and you agree on a start date. Keep your mailing campaign constantly up and running so that if any of those promising interviews go sour, you'll still have plenty of new ones in progress. And you'll proceed from a standing start.

A dedicated job campaign consisting of weekly mailings will yield far more interviews than merely responding to ads or networking. The more job interviews you get, the more likely it is you will get the job you want rather than a job you settled for.

CHAPTER 9

Your Pal: The Employment Application Form

I f you're like most people, you probably feel that filling out application forms before each interview is an imposition, especially if you're trying to downplay something in your employment history. It surely is, but the application form can be as much your friend as the employer's, even with its intrusive questions.

How carefully—or carelessly—you fill out a job application form tells the interviewer a lot about you in a hurry, especially if you're applying for clerical or administrative jobs. Employers will not entrust enormous quantities of information to which they attach much importance—files, records, reports, notes, memos, and spreadsheets—to a schlub who can't be bothered to properly fill out an application.

Furthermore, the application form is your chance to distinguish yourself from competitors who ignore or gloss over details on the form—unless they too are compulsively precise and follow directions to the letter. Here are some questions you may have when faced with those blank lines on an application form.

Question #1: Does an application blank show my personality?

Absolutely. Your interviewer can tell by reading the form how alert and cooperative you are (or how lazy and bored). It tells them how thorough you are, how neat, and how willingly you follow directions. The reasons you give for leaving past jobs tells how honest or inventive you are. If the interviewer can't decipher something you've scribbled or abbreviated, they may translate it to mean that you don't care a lot if you're understood.

Question #2: Those forms are so cut and dried,
where is there a chance for originality?

Where is there a chance for originality? There are *only* chances for original- ity. A survey of recruiting managers revealed that 35 percent of job applicants did not even slow down to write their last name first, as the form requested. So just following directions carefully is a virtue. Printing legibly so that every word is readable, even in a small space, is another.

Question #3: How else can I distinguish myself?

Write three brief comments in different sections on the application. Enclose each of the three in a circle so they'll get noticed. Comments such as, "Had highest one-day sales in dept.," shows you do your best even on temporary jobs. The second, "I work until the job is done," answers the question, "Would you be available for overtime?" The third comment, "A average in accounting courses," implies you are an A student. Capeesh? Employers hate reading applications almost as much as you hate filling them out. By making key points "pop" for them, you'll stand out.

Question #4: Anything else I can do to stand out?

Carry a fine-line red pen with you, just for this use. These short notes about results you've gotten previously may be the thing the interviewer remembers about you when you meet. It's a great feeling to have this happen. The following is a long list of practical hints you'll want to keep in mind when you tackle your next job application form. Read all directions *before starting to write.*

1. Use a fine-line pen. Spaces are often too small for the information they want.

2. Fill in all spaces if you want to show particular thoroughness. Write N/A (not applicable) in spaces you've left empty to show it was not from oversight.

3. Write "Open" in space asking "Salary Desired." Because employers are so used to it, this dodge probably won't work for very long, but it's a good place to start. Then you can move up to a salary *range.* (Please see Chapters 5 and 16 on handling salary questions.)

4. If you've held a job two years or longer, list only the years: 2001–05.

5. If you have held a job fewer than two years, use numbers for months: 9/99–4/01.

6. When listing names of former supervisors or references, omit titles: "Frank Brown," not "Mr. Frank Brown."

7. Add area codes before *all* phone numbers if you want to show thoroughness.

8. Show your highest level of education only. If you've been to college, no need to list the name and address of your high school. One exception is if you have a graduate degree, where you will probably want to include both your undergraduate and graduate education.

9. Fill out a sample application form at home and take it with you on interviews. You can get one in a stationery store. You won't have to pause for long, long minutes trying to recall obscure dates and addresses. You can breeze through the form in a third of the time it previously took.

In filling out applications, as with the rest of your job search, the underlying principle is this: *Everything* you write or say to an employer can be slanted to make you look good and stand out.

CHAPTER 10

What Really Counts in Business—and in Your Resume and Interview

Find them, fight them, defeat them, and move on.
—Credo of Ulysses S. Grant

A t the start of the Civil War, Ulysses S. Grant had retired from the army and was clerking in the family leather-goods store in Galena, Illinois. He applied for an army command, but was turned down—even though he was a graduate of West Point, one who had distinguished himself on the battlefield during the Mexican War. Grant persisted, however, and contacted the War Department and officers he knew from West Point and the war in Mexico. The War Department finally relented and gave Grant command of a regiment.

Within three years, Grant was commanding all the Union armies, over a million soldiers and 100 generals. Within seven years, Grant was president. If you look at the six factors below that really count in business, you'll find Grant had four of the six. While it's certainly no guarantee that the cultivation of these six factors will get you into the CEO's chair, the odds are steep that without a good portion of them, you won't make it anywhere.

The Six "What-Counts" Factors Mirror Management's Own Values

The following six What-Counts Factors are skills and character traits. They are not easily measured by tests. Yet they're the reason an employer will pick one resume over another from a pile. For companies with a special problem, the possession of a single What-Counts Factor with the power to solve that problem will propel your resume to the attention of decision-makers. Following each of the six factors are a couple of examples of how you would express that factor as an accomplishment.

What-Counts Factor #1: Build Profits and Create Wealth

Of all the motivations for hiring you, none is as strong as the profit motive. Peter Drucker, business guru and former professor of management at Claremont College, says, "The first performance requirement in a business is economic performance—profit." Executives also know that profits not only must rise annually, but that they must also grow faster than the competition. Here are three examples to show you the attention-getting power of the profit factor. These are employees who earn their cost back.

* "Created and developed the entire ESL program / built enrollment in the program from 35 students a semester to over 500 / built instructors from 4 to 30 / quadrupled income from tuition from $60,000 to $788,000 in three years."—*Resume of school academic director*

* "Started with zero base and built consulting income to $1.4 million."—*Resume of benefits administrator*

* "Built Rx daily volume from average of 30 a day to present 150–200 a day / dollar sales from $1,200 a week to present $17,000 per week."—*Resume of a pharmacy manager*

What-Counts Factor #2: Cut Waste

Costs never go down; they always go up. It's easier and faster to enlarge profits by cutting costs than it is to originate new profits. Cost-cutting requires only that you *stop* doing something. Stop employing 150 employees. Stop manufacturing in America. Stop hiring anyone over thirty. If you show through examples that you savagely hack away at fixed costs with a meat ax, and have a cash register where your heart should be, you can count on an enthusiastic reading of your resume. Don't just count on it, bet on it. Here are three easy examples of workers who cut costs:

* "Cut one day's time off the two days previously needed for a team of two to make floor inspections."—*Resume of senior credit administrator*

* "Bought and packaged store's own gift baskets for $25 v. $40 previously paid to wholesaler for similar baskets."—*Resume of retail salesperson*

* "Reduced food costs by 50 percent and increased the average check from $12 to $15."—*Resume of executive chef*

What-Counts Factor #3: Create/Exploit Change

Creating change is the path to leadership in or out of business. Change always presents opportunities, but many see it as a threat. Insecurity makes people resist change. It takes a skilled people-handler to effect change in a bureaucracy. You must overcome or move around all the bitterness, the turf battles, the in-fighting and pettiness so rife in many organizations. However, far more money is made by exploiting change than by creating it. *Creating* change can take a revolution. *Exploiting* change takes only innovation and thus occurs more often, as in these examples:

* "Cut head office staff from 68 to 10—an unprecedented step in this agency."—*Resume of regional small business administrator*

* "Reorganized three plants for continuous-flow manufacturing and J I T inventory / This changed the whole character of the company and its profitability."—*Resume of vice president, manufacturing*

* "Forecast that depressed economy would lead to more 2- to 3-day weekend trips, and fewer trips abroad . . . built duffel-type bags volume from $45,000 to over $600,000 and still rising."—*Resume of product manager*

Before we leave the No. 3 What-Counts Factor, we ought to observe that change is perilous. Change can be a disaster if you're ahead of your time. This may explain why so many people are content to be stuck in time when it comes to their work habits, and why effecting a change is such a phenomenal resume-builder.

What-Counts Factor #4: Handle People Skillfully

People-handling is a skill high on every top executive's list. The Young President's Organization listed "getting along with other people" as the number-one personality trait important to their success. Top executives spend 80 percent of their time talking with other people. If you're a deft people-handler, you're good at getting around resistance, and that's what counts most in cost cutting. Cost-cutting initiatives are not easy to achieve. They almost always encounter resistance and confrontation. Workers see them as a threat to their jobs. They may retaliate with insolence, costly slowdowns, or strikes. What do you do? Call in the marines? How can you show you're a deft people-handler? By demonstrating a profit-aiding perspective when you interact with other people, as in these examples:

* Sharing rewards voluntarily with others adopted by entire chain: "Started the practice of giving half the dollar amount of a 'Shopper's Report' money award ($100) to any employee who was singled out for extraordinary service or courtesy / previous manager kept entire award / this variation was adopted by Wendy's throughout the chain."—*Resume of a Wendy's store manager*

* Good people-handling skills bring hotel's guests back: "Always subtle, courteous, and poised with guests / received letter of commendation from hotel's general manager, given when an employee gets five or more unsolicited complimentary comments from hotel guests."—*Resume of hotel front-desk assistant*

* Good people-handling skills reduces employee turnover: "Replaced 80 percent of 15-person wait staff, retrained others, do not like to replace staff if they are receptive to retraining / very low turnover, two-thirds of our hires are still here after three years."—*Resume of executive chef*

Why Education Is Not One of the Six Factors

Education is important only at the entry level where employers demand it. But Dr. Lewis B. Ward of Harvard feels that companies hiring college graduates have been putting too much emphasis on high IQs and high grades. There is no correlation between intelligence and good judgment. A student can be book smart and have zero judgment. Shrewd judgment, knowing when to say yes and when to back away, skills for which the market offers big salaries, shows up after we leave school. *Fortune* magazine surveyed 1,700 top male executives and found that, although they had done better in college than the average of all males, only one in twenty (eighty-five out of 1,700) had made the Dean's List, graduated cum laude, summa cum laude, or was valedictorian.

What-Counts Factor #5: Demonstrate Competitiveness

Most salaried and hourly people do their job as well as it needs to be done but seldom go beyond that, unless the boss is watching. They're not competitive. Jobs do not come in search of them. What employers really want and hope for are those employees who exceed expectations. People who outperform. And how do you outperform? You simply work fifty minutes of every hour when those around you are working thirty and forty minutes.

Bosses are always impressed by the stupendous percentage increases that job applicants show on their resumes. It's really not a mystery. It's primarily because most bosses don't know how long it takes to perform any task, and (unless their workers are already on measured pay for performance) 90 percent of workers will work at about 40 to 70 percent of their energy level. If you have someone performing fifty minutes of every hour while the rest work between thirty and forty minutes of every hour, it isn't all that hard to be number one if you decide to be.

What-Counts Factor #6: Show Teamwork

The great merit in showing teamwork on your resume is that it's an indication of *adaptability*—an ability to follow orders, cooperate, and compromise without pitching a hissy fit or raising petty objections. Teamwork is not merely an aid to big organizations, it's an outright necessity. Just try getting by without it. Moreover, teams are easier to guide and control. As soon as you take a job, you become a member of a working team. Don't expect the team to adapt to you. It's up to you to become one of them.

Leapfrog, a developer and manufacturer of children's educational toys, took a big gamble. Over a four-year period, it pulled together over 300 engineers, designers, and consultants to bring the Fly to market, a talking computer pen for children ages eight to thirteen. Without teamwork, they could never have brought it off. The following are accomplishments that show the merit of teamwork:

* "Teamed with one other person to handle a very large project intended to shorten the response time in processing claims / cut response time by one-third."—*Resume of benefits specialist*

* "Developed with the engineering group company's state-of-the-art electronic chip and safeguarded it by securing worldwide patent protection."—*Resume of vice president of manufacturing*

* "Member of team that helped develop intelligence that led to arrest and conviction of Medicaid providers / at a savings to the state of New York of upwards of $15 million a year."—*Resume of social services specialist*

Just a Reminder

Nothing but results counts in a Mad Brute Resume. You're dealing with a large unseen audience of prospective employers. All of them aim to get far greater value from a prospective employee than they part with in salary and benefits. They will snub you if you look like another mouth to feed and invite you in if you are someone who earns their cost back. You'll give employers what is most likely to appeal to them if you show them one or more accomplishments in the six What-Counts Factors. I guarantee it.

CHAPTER 11

Overcoming the Big No: How to Deal with the Fear Factor

Perhaps the most dreaded part of finding a job is dealing with the rejections that inevitably come with the process. It feels personal. After all, you spent long hours on that cover letter and resume. You rehearsed answers to interview questions. It seemed to work. They acted as if they liked you during the interview, as if they were going to invite you to join their little family. You waited by the phone, convinced an offer was on the way. Then . . . nothing. You wait. You go over your answers in your head. You start to second-guess yourself. You call to follow up but suddenly the boss that courted you only days or weeks earlier is acting like you've got a case of the Shanghai flu. You try to rally, convinced you still have a chance, even as your hopes start to plummet. You go to the mailbox. A rejection letter is waiting.

Avoid the Dangers of Projection

There is not a single topic that causes more heartache than *projection*. Please note that word well. Projection is the belief that something is yours now, when it is merely a possibility. Not even a probability, just a possibility. Read the stories of the people below and see if you have been, or are becoming like them, in your job search.

One of our New York City resume-writing customers, Julian Kahn, had just concluded successful interviews with two employers. He told me he stayed home waiting for his two prospects to phone him, telling him he was needed and wanted and asking when he could start. He was certain they would call him back. One of them said they would fix it with the union so he would not have to join. Julian took this confidence-sharing to mean he was in. While he waited, he mused about which job would be a better fit for him, comparing and contrasting advantages and responsibilities. It was great fun as his mind romped from one job to the other.

Except that neither of the two employers ever called. Either Julian read too much into what the employers said to him in their interviews, or maybe they meant what they said but later changed their minds about him. Julian was so hurt and seething with resentment he decided to fly to Houston where he heard there were more jobs. The two turndowns crushed Julian. He began to feel he was not good enough, instead of feeling that he had made it as a contender. He sat at home brooding and watching television for weeks. His job campaign apparently did not allow for turndowns from *projections.*

Helen, another client, mailed a cover letter and resume directly to one of the nation's biggest banks inquiring about a teller's job. A month later, they called her in for an interview (she had three). She was invited to an orientation that included a dozen other hopefuls. Afterward, an assistant manager came over to Helen and told her how impressed they all were with her bearing. He said he was referring her to the district manager, and he called her at home after the interview with the district manager to ask how it went. The district manager told Helen everyone was abuzz over her, and assured her he would call within forty-eight hours. Ten insufferable days crawled by while Helen waited by the phone, waiting to hear from those who held her success in their hands. On the tenth day, she got a letter with a wrong first name, telling her she was no longer in their thoughts. But . . . anyway . . . thanks for thinking about us.

The lesson here is potential employers may call for you in a cab but send you home on foot. Once they decide against you, then it's FORGET YOU! When a person is no longer a contender, employers immediately give them the proverbial cold shoulder. Prepare for employers to be totally indifferent to runners-up. They may like you, *and tell you so in interview(s),* but then hire someone else whom they like even more. The bank may have kept Helen on hold till their first choice was on board, a common practice. (Later in this chapter, we'll see how it is that an employer's second, third, or even fourth choice sometimes gets the job.)

In cases like these, it's normal to feel despondent and sad. You may feel used, unwanted, and as if everyone else is better. Or maybe you'll get angry and want to call the employer and give them a piece of your mind. Who wouldn't feel this way? No one likes to feel they were led on or lied to. What you have to do to is be stern with yourself: Make *projecting* itself unlawful. Don't indulge in it. If an interview goes well, refuse to let yourself think about it—until and if it results in a job offer. Work hard, expect much, but when you've said your piece and the interview is over, fuhgeddaboutit, and send off five more cover letters and resumes. Your happiness will immediately increase tenfold.

Make Sure the Job Offer You Get Is Real

EMPLOYER: "We feel you're the person we've been looking for, and *we want you*. How soon can you start?"

That is an offer.

Realize that an inexperienced, flattering, or sympathetic interviewer can lead you on with beautiful non-offers like these:

"You sound like you were made for this job. I'm going to set up another interview for you with one of my colleagues." Realize that, while 70 percent of second interviews lead to job offers, 30 percent don't.

Similarly beware of, "You did nicely in your interview with Mr. Brown . . . we're very interested."

It's easy to get a little praise and think you're in. You think all your problems are solved. Not so fast. You can just as easily call back on the appointed date and hear, "Oh, we're very sorry, but we've decided to delay filling that position for a while."

Or, "Another candidate we saw after you had better credentials . . . thanks for coming in . . . we'll keep your resume on file in the event something opens up."

Or you'll open your mailbox hopefully and get their printed form letter telling you, "We enjoyed meeting you, but we gave the job to somebody more impressive."

It's just enough recognition that you can go on suffering instead of dying. Meantime, you've been sitting by your phone, going nail-biting crazy waiting to hear from them. You've even given up on setting new interviews. You've stopped answering ads. You've alerted all your friends with your sudden exuberance. You may even have planned a short vacation before starting work. All because you *projected* that you were as good as employed when you were still only a contender.

Whatever you do, keep up your momentum! Don't stop interviewing and sending out more resumes just because you've had a very promising interview. Solicit more than one job at a time. And when you finish an interview without a job offer or an offer of a second visit, write it off mentally as a possibility, *not a probability*.

The great danger in projecting is that you set yourself up for a *big* letdown if what you are projecting does not happen, which is most of the time, or at least a lot of times. So don't kid yourself. If you kid yourself into thinking their flattery translates into a job offer, remember that an interviewer may *like* you but may still not *hire* you. Interviewers base a final job offer on all sorts of variables. They weigh input from all sorts of people within the company. Rapport may not be the tipping point, so don't invest too much stock in it.

What Have You Got to Lose?

Almost all responses to classified ads are turned away for one reason. *The applicant does not meet all the requirements* set forth in the ad. Nevertheless, most job searchers still apply to ads for which they are only partially qualified. Maybe the ad lists six requirements, and you meet only five. As mentioned in Chapter 2, that is a *reach*.

If you send your resume to five reaches, it's possible that you may not get a single response if a machine is doing the first reading. If you send your resume to a big company, it's a given that it will be prescreened by a machine. Wynn Resorts, Las Vegas, looked to hire 8,000 card dealers, housekeepers, waitresses, parking attendants, and other workers for their new billion-dollar hotel-and-casino complex. Rather than reading through 150,000 resumes, the Wynn people hired an online staffing company, Recruitmax Software, to help them with the initial online screenings.

Large employers who may get a thousand or more responses to an ad use electronic resume screeners. They program these machines to reject any resume that doesn't meet the requirements for an open position. If you mail to smaller employers who actually open their own mail and read everything, you stand a far better chance with your reach response. If your other achievements are sufficiently striking, an employer may waive a requirement for you. That's what reach responses hope for.

If you mail in your resume with a what-have-I-got-to-lose attitude, you will not be distraught that you did not get a response. Disappointed maybe, but not tragically so. That's the way it ought to be for your own happiness and peace of mind.

Tactics for Overcoming the Fear of Rejection

The mere *fear* of rejection, being shown the door, is the single biggest obstacle facing job-hunters.

We dread being made to feel like damaged merchandise. A few rejections in a row can crush our feelings of self-worth. We start to look upon turndowns as proof that we're pretty crappy. Self-confidence bleeds out of us. Let an interviewer remain silent for a few moments, and we're ready to drop through the floor with anxiety. It's all quite explainable. Sigmund Freud tells us that any fear so strong that it keeps us from doing what we want to do is called a phobia. It's named for Phobus, son of Ares, who in Greek mythology could implant fear in armies and cause their defeat. Freud advanced the concept that we form phobias to shield us from what troubles us. For instance, let's say you feel guilty about being out of a job. Each time an interviewer asks you if you are presently working, you feel profoundly embarrassed and regret taking the interview.

The result is that you develop a phobia toward job interviews as a defense against feeling worthless. You stop sending out resumes. This has the undesired side effect of stopping your job search campaign cold. You sullenly join 3 million other Americans as an employment statistic of the U.S. Department of Labor, in the category "People Who Are Too Discouraged to Look for Work."

In his book, *Stop Running Scared,* Dr. Herbert Fensterheim says that persistent fear of an object or idea that originally does not justify fear usually prepares you for the three Fs: flight, fight, or freeze. The surprising thing about all this is how many people don't realize how much they fear rejection—"The Big No."

Just to show how subtle fear of rejection can be, here is an actual account that is rather typical.

In the offices of the Forty Plus Executives Club of New York, a support group for out-of-work executives forty and older, is John S., fifty-seven, an executive salesperson in industrial sales. John recounts how he once took his resume to a large industrial park with the notion that he would make cold job-hunting calls on presidents of companies in the $30- to $100-million sales range.

"I braced myself to face the dragon ladies [receptionists]," John recalls, "but I was so surprised to find them all so agreeable, even offering me coffee. I saw two presidents in an hour versus two personnel people in the previous two weeks. I went out whistling."

On the third, fourth, and fifth calls, John was asked to leave a resume, but he got the name of the hiring person. On the sixth call, John was told, "He will see you only by appointment," and on the seventh call the receptionist brushed him off with, "We're not looking for anyone now." John thereupon quit for the day, although it was only a little past noon. Asked why, John said, "I don't know why, I just was no longer in the mood to knock on doors." When it was suggested that he feared further rejections, John sheepishly smiled and said, "As a salesman, I'm embarrassed to say yes."

Fear-Maintaining Escape Behavior

Dr. Fensterheim calls such job-interview avoidance "fear-maintaining escape behavior." You can't keep the fright from occurring, so you avoid the upsetting event that brings it on. You keep finding excuses not to seek out more interviews. Thus, you don't give yourself a chance to find out that what you fear may not happen at all. As a result, you keep yourself unemployed, and your fear remains alive. According to Dr. Fensterheim, you rearrange your life to cope with your fear. "At some point," he counsels, "You have to take a stand and face your fear. You can then begin to run your life out of choice and not out of fear. It all lies in one sentence: Face your fear."

Facing Your Fear

In my survey of 500 executives, I asked each one if fear of rejection was the biggest obstacle to getting the job a person is qualified for. Only 37 percent agreed. That's a surprisingly low figure and does not back up in the slightest the general statistic for all job hunters.

Then it hit me! The people surveyed were all high achievers. They had risen to high positions—chairmen, president, vice president, department head—precisely because they didn't fear rejection. They had a far lower level of anxiety about job interviews than did most other job seekers. Or they had no fear at all. "I never went to an interview expecting to be rejected," said a marketing director of a science magazine. An export manager of a large chemical company said, "Rejection is a reality in business and personal relationships, so we might as well get used to it." "I always adopted the philosophy that I would give the interview my best shot and hope it was sufficient to get the job," said the quality-control manager of a pharmaceutical company, "but if it wasn't, rejection might be temporarily disappointing, but I've never looked at it as an obstacle."

Battling Back

These executives refused to allow turndowns to trigger fear reactions. They knew that rarely do jobs come in search of talent, and turndowns are inevitable, which helps to explain their upward progress. Scott Budge, of the counseling center at Pace University, runs a weekly support group for out-of-work executives in New York City. He says the *social stigma* of being jobless weighs heavily on out-of-work job hunters. "Our whole life," Budge says, "is spent preparing for work or leaving it. The only acceptable nonworking periods are schooling, vacations, and retirement."

The greatest taboo next to being out of work, we are taught, is *moving down*. It's the chief no-no among no-no's. You must grow. Faster. Bigger. Higher. Stronger. Wealthier. You must go ever upward. At the Forty Plus Club, the most horrifying thought is the consideration of having to move down in one's career or financial status. Such an attitude will slow down your job hunt by keeping you from looking for realistic alternatives.

What Triggers the Fear Factor?

"The greater the desperation, the greater the fear of rejection becomes," says E. Patricia Birsner, author of *Job Hunting for the 40 Plus Executive,* who has worked with hundreds of out-of-work executives. The fear of being unprepared for embarrassing questions often triggers the flight, fight, or freeze response. Birsner recalls the suffering of a female executive who was fired because she had loaned her company credit card to her son. "She was so stunned at being fired," Birsner says, "that she simply couldn't answer the question, 'Why did you leave your last job?'" Once you learn how to handle these questions, she says, you won't feel nearly so scared, and after a while you'll answer them with poise and confidence. Loaning the credit card to her son was a mistake of judgment. She regrets it mightily now. It won't happen ever again. Now it's time to move on.

Worrying About How It Will Look

What *are* you so afraid of? Do you see the interviewer as an authority figure from your past? Are you embarrassed because you're applying for a job for which you are overqualified? Or because you're between jobs? Been in jail? Got fired? Aging? Too short? Too heavy? Dropped out? Never graduated from college? The list goes on. You should realize it isn't the interviewer but your response to the mental question, "How will it look?" that makes you feel anxious and insecure. If you allow your fear of the Big No to become your enemy, it will destroy you. If you learn to neutralize it, then nothing will stop you from pursuing the job you want.

Facing Fear: Eight Guidelines to Ward off Rejection Fears

Here are eight tips for keeping a paralyzing fear of rejection at bay:

1. **Depersonalize the interview.** Employers may get as many as 500 to 1,000 resumes for one job opening. How can you and the other 499 runners-up be no good?

2. **Don't make it all or nothing**. Don't set yourself up for a letdown. Tell yourself, "The job could be mine, it's a good possibility, it's certainly not an impossibility."

3. **Don't blame the interviewer**. Realize that interviewers aren't in a hurry to think and behave as you would like. Blame your turndown on a hard-hearted interviewer who didn't like you, and you will learn nothing from the process.

4. **Don't live in the past.** When you dredge up past career or job-hunting failures prior to your interview, your nervous system kicks into high

gear, and you experience all the emotions that go with those disappointments all over again.

5. **Don't get mad at the system.** Is there any less pleasurable experience in the world than job-hunting? Still, you must adjust to the world rather than expecting the world to adjust to you. The easiest thing is to conform to what 130 million other people are putting up with.

6. **Take the spotlight off yourself.** Sell your skills, not yourself. Concentrate on what you're there for, to find the interviewer's problems and show how you both can work together to solve them.

7. **See yourself in the new role.** Form a mental picture of the positive self you'd like to become in job interviews, rather than focusing on what scares you.

8. **Keep your sense of humor high.** Nobody yet has been shot or banished or jailed for not pleasing a job interviewer.

Change a Bad Attitude

It's easy to let rejection color your attitude after a while. Why you do or don't get a certain job isn't always logical or fair. And as much as you should try to treat employers (even those who reject you) with professionalism and courtesy, they won't always return the favor. No one can blame you for experiencing feelings of negativity. However, employers have a sixth sense when it comes to sniffing out candidates they think will be a problem. If you find your attitude heading south, it's time to adopt some strategies on how to shift your perspective.

In general terms, an attitude is a set of beliefs that a person holds. The beliefs may be obvious or hidden, positive or negative. Studies have shown that positive attitudes help you learn faster and better. Negative attitudes slow learning. The following situations demonstrate this.

Did you ever notice how quickly someone will learn a phone number when there are romantic possibilities involved? Conversely, have you ever noticed how difficult it is for some people to remember a dentist appointment?

Having a positive attitude toward getting a good job involves what is called "positive self-talk":

1. I can get any job I am qualified for.

2. I can enjoy the interview's give-and-take and not be nervous.

3. I know a great deal already about the company, and I intend to learn a great deal more.

4. This job will improve my life in many ways.

5. If I don't get this job, there are plenty more out there.

Having this attitude will help you get along with the interviewer, to be patient, to endure stress and disappointments, and to succeed in the end.

The chief obstacle most people create for themselves is that they harbor a negative attitude towards their chances of success, or an attitude that wavers between hope and despair. Some people seem to have a special knack for getting jobs, while for others it presents an impossible challenge. The truth is that everybody can land a job if they set their minds to it and have a positive attitude.

Everyone starts life with a positive attitude. Somewhere along the way a negative attitude may develop. This negative attitude is accompanied by negative self-talk. Some people begin saying to themselves, "I can't get hired because I'm not good enough . . . Who would want me, I only have a high school education . . . Everybody else is better . . . Maybe today is not such a good day to look . . . Really, why should I even bother?" They convince themselves that they're unwanted because they've convinced themselves they're poor job candidates.

If you have a negative attitude toward getting a job, you can solve the problem. Attitudes can be changed. You can talk yourself into having a positive attitude by changing negative self-talk to positive self-talk. Here's an example. You might start saying to yourself:

1. Starting right now, I'm going to become a smarter job-hunter and better all parts of my life.

2. I'm more capable than many people who are more successful than I.

3. I'll reach for the success I know I can achieve.

4. I'm going to discover and change whatever obstacles are causing my negative attitudes.

5. If I can't outthink them, I can outwork them.

6. If others can get good jobs, so can I. I'm not a quitter; I don't give up.

7. I'll do whatever it takes to succeed.

It's good to repeat positive self-talk *often*. It's a true and proven motivator and will lead you to success eventually. Repetition, they say, is the mother of learning.

Turning Negative Self-Talk Around

Imagined risks are only in a person's mind. Another name for imagined risks is *negative self-talk*. Here are some imagined risks (negative talk) and alongside them is offsetting positive talk you can use to counter the negative phrases.

I can't start a conversation with him. What if he asks me why I left my job?
Most interviewers know times are tough in my industry; some certainly may be empathic.

If I say anything at this meeting, I'll make a fool of myself. No one will ever forget it.
Most people will respect me for making a suggestion even if they disagree with me.

If I give in on this, everyone will think I'm wishy-washy and without strong convictions.
Compromising now will show I'm flexible, willing to listen carefully and give to get.

This is just one more piece of work given to me because the others say no, and I'm as busy as they are.
This is a chance for me to show I can help out wherever help is needed and handle greater responsibility.

Asking for help now will make people think I can't handle the job.
If I ask for help, team members will know I want to do a good job.

She is so much better than I am. I can't talk to her about the problem.
She might be good at this, but there are other things I'm good at. I'll just give it a try and discuss the problem with her.

I'm not sure I can handle this. I'd better quit right now.
Quitting won't get me anywhere. If I give it my best try, who knows; I might succeed.

How a Positive Attitude Affects Your Career

Confidence in your skills is good, but remember this: *The ability to do a job exceptionally well is still only one part of a successful career.* Other qualities are also needed, and most of these are *people* skills, such as getting along with fellow workers and your superiors. Having a positive attitude improves your people skills. When you have highly developed people skills, it lubricates the way for you to progress to better-paying jobs.

We can't see, hear, or touch our attitudes because they're inside our heads. Even so, attitudes influence our behavior, especially the way we communicate with others. Our attitudes make themselves known to others when we speak, write, use body language, or go silent.

Because people speak so much more often than they write, attitudes play a much more important role in spoken language than in written language. Attitudes greatly influence the hidden messages that we express when we speak. These hidden messages can be positive or negative.

Attitudes also affect how we interpret what other people say. If we want to maintain good human relations, we must be aware of how attitudes affect our spoken conversation. Attitudes reflect lasting feelings about people, objects, issues, and events. By lasting, we mean the feelings tend to remain unchanged for long periods of time, in contrast to moods, which may change quickly and often.

Maintaining a Positive Attitude

A positive attitude doesn't happen by accident. First, you must adopt the habit of looking on the bright side when things happen that cause others around you to be negative. During the Great Depression, most people only remembered that 30 percent of the workforce was unemployed. They overlooked the fact that even in the worst of times, 70 percent of Americans were still working, paying their bills, and moving on.

People who have a positive attitude toward work are effective, efficient, and productive. Because they have a positive attitude, they enjoy their work and feel good about what they do. A negative attitude toward life or work lessens productivity. Unhappy people with bad attitudes are usually neither efficient nor effective. They often don't reach their goals. For these people, work is a burden. Their negative attitudes affect their work energy and the others around them. They get bored easily and operate at no more than 40 to 70 percent of their energy level.

You may think that there is much involved in changing an attitude. There really isn't. If you maintain a positive attitude and work harder than the next person toward your goals, you'll develop a *winning* attitude. However, if you chronically fill your mind with negative self-talk, you reduce your productivity and hurt your chances of success in all areas of your life. In each case, you must say to yourself, "This is the attitude I choose to have."

It Doesn't Matter If You're the First Choice, as Long as You're the Final One

We began this chapter by talking about how dangerous it is to project that just because you really want a job, you are going to get it. You need to treat all job prospects as possibilities, not certainties.

The other, more hopeful side of the coin is this: Just because it appears that you won't be getting a job offer, never assume that all hope is lost. The reality is that you still may be under consideration, even weeks after you thought the job must have been given to somebody else. Very possibly, the position has been offered to—but not accepted by—other candidates, and your turn is coming next.

It happens all the time: Second, third, and even fourth choices wind up with the job. Only the interviewer knows it. The person chosen is always allowed to believe they were the first choice, so they'll have no troubling doubts later. This will also help you understand why you often will get a job offer weeks after you may have given up hope. The scenario is usually predictable.

Their first choice for the current job opening is some fantastic human. But he is also the first choice elsewhere, and their higher offer wins him. Drat! So they call number two in line.

Number Two is no slouch either. But she decides after two interviews that this job is not what she thought it was and, with that self-confidence of someone who already has a job, she turns them down flat. Forget her! On to the third choice.

Number Three goes for the job. He accepts the offer, turns in his notice, and lo and behold! His present boss makes him a counteroffer no one in his senses would refuse. (Refer to Chapter 15 for provisos on accepting counteroffers.) These turndowns hit your interviewer like three hammer blows to the chest. "Look here! I'm not going through this mind-numbing interviewing all over again . . . I've been at it for weeks . . . the job needs to be filled . . . who else is there?"

Just then, *your* resume parachutes into view. They now recall you smiling up at them and telling them as you got up to leave, "I'll never let you down," which is what they feel these three other applicants have done. Again they go over your resume, line by line. You appear to be a doer and achiever, with measured accomplishments at every job you've had. Nothing in your resume offends them. They reach for the phone. They dial. They leave a message on your answering machine—as you remember, you're not picking up the phone when it might be a employer—to please call them back as soon as you can. It happens all the time.

CHAPTER 12

The Right Way to Bounce Back from Unemployment

Chains of gold can be the hardest of all to throw off. With unemployment checks being mailed to your door, you are getting paid to sit home, rest, and be lazy. Job hunting? Sure, you send out some resumes, go to an interview . . . and then go see a movie. You have a rationalization for spending money without earning any: They kicked you out, now you can kick them back by collecting unemployment, which they are obligated by law to contribute to. Thirty-nine weeks of freedom from oppression. You may be free, but it's worthless if you are restless and stressed because you know what you really should be doing.

Resilience Can Be Developed

Just as loafing around is a learned habit, so is resilience—the ability to bounce back. How long do you have to search for a job? How long should you persevere? Until the no's stop.

Psychologists tell us that resilience is neither rare nor an inborn quality; consequently, most people have the potential to develop resilience. "A resilient person may suffer physical and emotional pain and go through tremendous financial difficulty and uncertainty, but he or she is able to bounce back," reports psychologist Byron Egelund, who has studied several hundred high-risk children living in families battered by poverty, drugs, and abuse.

The key to resilience is knowing that something you've done is good. Marina Pisano, a reporter for the *San Antonio Express News,* writes that resilient people have one or more of the following six protective factors working for them:

1. Problem-solving ability

2. Competence in some area

3. Self-esteem

4. High motivation

5. Alertness to the world outside

6. Strong supportive connections in life

You may find that one or more of the above factors are natural with you, and one or more of the others can be learned with training. As you look over the six factors, it may cause you to be more reflective about your own attitudes and competencies, not necessarily a bad thing.

Beware of the Danger Zone

Unemployment is a bad situation, but you will make it worse by doing little or nothing to find a job until the last unemployment check is only a week or two away. It's then you'll commit the fatal mistake—making career decisions out of desperation. At that point, you need to get on someone's payroll, anyone's payroll, *fast*, so you settle instead of reaching. You take a job beneath your abilities. And more than likely, you find yourself back out on the job market before you know it.

One of the major errors people make when they're suddenly unemployed, whether they're skilled or unskilled, is to say, "Okay, I'll take a vacation." They feel they'll get a job easily on their return or that they need a breather to recover from the shock of a layoff or termination. Such a move is simply procrastination and an attempt to put off the drudgery of hunting for a new job. If people do not find work easily, their condition of unemployment begins what Richard Price, professor of psychology at the University of Michigan, calls "a chain of adversity." This chain of adversity can include marital tension, psychological stress, and other problems not immediately tied to loss of income. According to Professor Price: "The first thing people don't understand about job loss is that it isn't the job loss that gets you, it's the cascade of negative life events that follow." He cites examples such as the inability to send a child to college, the loss of health benefits, or the inability to make car or mortgage payments. If your car is repossessed because you can't afford the payments, you have also lost the means to look for a job. Then you suddenly find that you can't sell your house because everyone else in the neighborhood is unemployed. It's like hunger married to thirst. The loss of a job begins a downward spiral of negative events.

It's never a good idea to fall back on unemployment. A long absence from the workplace usually must be explained. Why were you out of work for thirty-nine weeks? This will lead the list of questions you will be asked when you again start looking for work. Consider that 3.6 million Americans ran out of unemployment benefits in 2004, the most in thirty years. About 1.8 million Americans—one in five—have been unemployed for six months or longer, according to statistics from the U.S. Department of Labor.

If you take a vacation instead of looking for a job, what it means is that you just don't want to go out and face the possible rejection every job-hunter alive faces every time he makes a call. Dwelling too much on your situation becomes an escape from action to avoid rejection. Just do it. Send out the resumes. Pound the pavement. Develop tenacity, stick-to-it-iveness.

Job-hunting is hard, but you need to put it in perspective. You probably do other things you don't like to do because you know that they are the right thing to do—like sticking to a diet, or paying your monthly credit card debt, or calculating and paying your taxes. If you find yourself getting stuck, refer to Chapter 11, titled "Overcoming the Big No." It'll help you develop the right attitude to shake off the desperation and keep on looking.

CHAPTER 13

The Truth About How Employment Agencies Really Work

Y ou'll want to know these three basic facts about employment agencies if you are working with them during the course of your job search:

1. The *employer,* not the job applicant, is their client and the one who pays their fee.

2. They are probably the best source for entry-level jobs.

3. They place about one in twenty applicants who come to them.

How the Agencies Work

Let's say you are Emily Able, and I run Miss Katherine's Employment Agency. You've just graduated from Aplex Business Institute with a degree in business management. Our agency's ads in the Sunday classifieds never fail to list alluring jobs for administrative assistants with high-status organizations, regardless of how bleak the current job market may be. And that's what brings you to me.

Courtesy with a Motive

I size you up with my avid, all-seeing gaze and mentally grade you *salable* (someone likely to impress an employer and draw a job offer). My job now is to place you before you sign up with another agency or get a job on your own. If you're attractive to us, you'll be equally desirable to others. I take pains to flatter and please and accommodate you. I can be oh-so-friendly and polite and generously reassuring when it's profitable to be so. Just as I can be remote and arch and unreachable by phone with applicants I judge unsalable.

Next, I call around to the agency's clients. These are usually large organizations with twenty layers of management, and they're always hiring someone. I tell them, "I have Emily here, someone who seems to possess real merit, someone I feel would definitely be a real treasure to add to your payroll. May I send her right over before someone else snaps her up?"

Safety First (Last and Always)

What I am really selling my client—how to put this—is not Emily Able but me. My imprimatur is *a form of reassurance, an extra margin of safety the client needs in case higher-ups should later question the hiring*. They know from experience they will not endanger their own job in any way by hiring someone our agency has screened and tested. They know I won't send them an underperformer or a doofus who would bring water to a river. They quite likely may improve their own reputation for hiring efficient workers by selecting my choices.

So far so good, and it gets better. You, Emily, now have something from me that makes you all the more hirable: our agency's endorsement. Our backing and support. If one of our clients does not have an immediate opening, I'll keep calling others until I place you. My livelihood depends on placing you as quickly as possible before someone else sees how capable you are and snatches you from us.

Commonly Asked Questions about Agencies

You may ask, if I'm so marketable, what do I need an employment agency for? And why do employers need you if they have such fascinating jobs open? Employment agencies know about job openings that are never advertised—remember, only 12 to 15 percent of job openings are advertised. They also know about jobs that are *about to open* because someone retired, got a promotion, quit, is not coming back from maternity leave, got fired, is moving to California, or simply died, as people do.

Employers use the agency for *initial* screening only. The employer can remain invisible and be spared the necessity of answering follow-up phone calls from eliminees, people they never want to see again. This is one of the reasons organizations run blind ads (ads that ask you to respond to a post-office box number). As the maxim tells us, cream rises to the top, and it's just the cream that employers want to hire. Or maybe an employer wants to do something forbidden, or not strictly illegal, and depends on the agency's greed for business to help carry it out with shifty dodges that don't break the law. For example, maybe the fantastic company in question wants to hire only slender, attractive assistants, or they don't want to hire a single parent with six kids who will use the company benefits for all they're worth.

Any tips on impressing them? Coming right up. Rule number one in dealing with employment agencies is this: Behave with them as you would with an employer who could say yes to you on the spot. They stand between you and the employer. If you don't wow them, you have a better chance of meeting the pope than any client of theirs. They have a reputation to sustain. Their reputation for picking competent, safe people is on the line with every candidate they dispatch.

Intend to be the most dazzling creature who has ever walked through their door or ever graced their desk with a resume. In entry-level positions, a smile of friendliness and good manners can take the place of experience. Arrange not to be among the first to be interviewed—Monday is the worst possible day of the week to present yourself. Readers of the Sunday ads rush in Monday morning and get equally rushed handling by agency interviewers. Make your appointment for Tuesday, when the crowd thins out and the atmosphere is more relaxed. You'll find you get more attention, longer. It's also a good strategy to drop by on Fridays. On Friday, agency people already know of job openings they will be advertising on Sunday.

Do You Need a Job Coach?

An employment agency can give your job search a boost by getting you into interviews, but they won't be going along to them with you. You may find that you could also benefit from some further instruction in what you should do once you're sitting in that chair opposite your potential future employer. In the

Broadway musical *A Funny Thing Happened on the Way to the Forum,* a character sings "Everybody Ought to Have a Maid." The same could be said about interview coaching; everybody ought to have it. The job market is increasingly competitive. Since it is the interview that brings the job offer, it makes sense to add the cost of job-coaching as a necessary expense of the chase.

I once had a mock interview that was filmed and shown to me later. The interview lasted fifteen minutes, and I was then shown the results on a television screen. I was disappointed to see myself sometimes looking off into the distance as I talked, or stumbling over answers to questions I hadn't anticipated, or seeming very nervous at some questions. I *thought* I was a poised applicant, but the film showed I was hesitant, nervous, and self-conscious, which I sometimes am.

Many people with a wide range of professional backgrounds, such as psychologists and professional resume-writers, have become job coaches on the side. Certification as a job coach is often easy to come by, and coaches may have limited coaching experience. That doesn't mean they aren't competent, but neither does it qualify them, in most cases, to charges fees of $100 per hour. A low-cost option is to have a trusted friend ask you interview questions while they film you with a home video camera. Even that simple exercise will show you where you need to brush up on your interviewing skills.

If, after trying to remedy your interviewing handicaps, you still find yourself coming up short, you should definitely consider working with an interview coach. They may be pricey, but so is long-term unemployment. Speaking and deporting yourself well are skills that you can use even after you get the job. Just be sure to work with someone reliable. I think that no more than $75 an hour is enough to charge a college student or lower-level job applicant, and even $50 is fair. With executive types, they can afford to pay some part of the princely sums they earn. Moreover, if you practice diligently at home what you have been taught by the coach, one or two sessions ought to be enough.

CHAPTER 14

Executive Recruiting: The Job Hunt in Reverse

E xecutive recruiting (head hunting, in slang terms) is the job-hunting process in reverse; the employer with an open position chases after you. But only a select and pampered few ever get the call. Here are the answers to the most frequently asked questions you may have about executive recruiting.

Question #1: How do I make the cut?

An employer hires a recruiter and asks the recruiter to find an executive to match the requirements of a very specific job opening. The executive sought is very likely doing the exact job for another employer at that very moment, and will be a master at it. But that's not the whole story. The target candidate will also be someone who makes an identifiable contribution to company profits, has an attractive business personality, and who has moved up the management ranks and is still rising. Salaries for typical candidates may start around $100,000 and go on into the millions.

Question #2: How is the recruiter paid?

The recruiter is retained and paid by the employer, usually about 30 percent of the salary and benefits the open position will pay. Moreover, the fee is not refundable to the employer should they elect not to hire any of the candidates uncovered by their recruiter. This fact distinguishes the retained recruiter from the ordinary run-of-the-mill employment agents who pose as executive recruiters. The theory is that by making the upfront payment nonrefundable if the client does not care for any of the candidates submitted, the recruiter will be able to be objective and seek the very best candidates. Many of the large executive recruiting firms are listed on the New York Stock Exchange and have annual revenues in the tens of millions.

Question #3: Would an executive recruiter be interested in me?

Executive recruiters successfully place about 10,000 highest-level executives a year out of about 750,000 executive job changes annually. As you can see, the odds are seventy-five to one against you. You can do better than that by handling things yourself.

Question #4: What types of applicants do executive recruiters not pay much attention to?

Recent college graduates with little job experience. Ordinary executives or managers who are merely competent. And especially not sought are out-of-work executives who are no longer rising up the corporate ranks. Out-of-work executives circulate their resumes to the very people who hire the executive recruiter. So, the recruiter avoids out-of-work candidates to avoid the embarrassment of sending in a resume the client already has rejected. Executive recruiters, as a rule, are not interested in out-of-work executives who have been displaced by a general layoff. There are just too many potential candidates out there who are young and rising and not looking for a change. Fresh faces.

Question #5: Would I be squandering my time writing to executive recruiters?

Many executive recruiters say they examine every resume they receive in the mail. But, in reality, they prefer to choose candidates from their own select files of eligible candidates. Some prestigious executive recruiting firms maintain files on over 100,000 rising executives in many industries. Others specialize in a single industry, such as fashion, advertising, or financial services. If you're a person of importance in your field, you very likely are already in their files.

The best strategy is not to mass mail a list of recruiters. There are several thousand, and you might spend $500 or more on a partial mailing with no results. Better to tackle the sources of job openings mentioned in Chapter 8, where the odds of your getting hired at a job you want are a more manageable one interview for every six resumes mailed.

It's a very heady sensation to pick up your home phone one night and find an executive recruiter at the other end. If you are one of the select few the recruiter calls, don't be too cocky or standoffish. If you appear out of reach, you may find the recruiter looking at someone else instead. Moreover, don't bite the hand that could feed you someday. Relationships with recruiters are valuable. Just because you may not presently be looking or the opportunity they're presenting isn't appealing, don't blow them off. You may need them someday when your present situation becomes stale.

If you really think you are a likely candidate to receive an executive recruiter's phone call, then one of the very best books to read on the subject is *The Career Makers,* by John R. Sibbald.

CHAPTER 15

The Danger in Accepting a Counteroffer

Whether it's through your own contacts, an employment agency, or an executive recruiter, you receive an offer for a job that pays well above your current position. Life is beautiful, and your choice is clear, right?

Maybe not. Consider this scene. You've just gotten that nice job offer, and you said, "Yes, I'll be there with bells on." You shake hands with your future boss and speed back to your present job. You turn in your notice to your boss. To your surprise, he makes you a counteroffer that is hard for someone who needs money as badly as you do to refuse.

Do you:

* Accept your boss's counteroffer?

* Say no to your boss's counteroffer?

* Ask for time to think it over?

That depends. If you hate your boss, then you must decide if you like money more than you hate your boss, in which case you will say yes and accept your boss's counteroffer. They (your present boss and your prospective boss) would, of course, know instantly from your affirmative answer that you are a person who can be bought, first, by your prospective boss, then again by your present boss. Your only loyalty is to yourself.

On the other hand, if you're really turned on by the new position—new office, new faces, more chances to shine, more money, a new beginning—then you'll likely turn down the boss's counteroffer with a grateful thanks, but no thanks.

Asking for time to think it over is always a smart move—*any time* you get an offer. You can set up a meeting with your boss after you've had a chance to gather your thoughts and express that there are considerations besides the money issue. Then, if you wish, you can ask for something beyond money. More office space. An extra week's vacation. An assistant. Flextime. Remember, when a boss says, "I want you," that's the time to push for whatever else you can get.

Here's the Problem If You Accept the Counteroffer . . .

Whether or not you stay in your present job, your boss may be upset with you. If they grant you this raise, how soon until you become restless again? Maybe they will start seeking your replacement as soon as you accept their counteroffer.

If you stay, it'll affect whether they still view you as being worthy of promotion. You obviously aren't dedicated to your relationship with them, the company that hired you and has paid your wages for months or even years. The higher up the ladder you are, the more limiting it will be to your future growth in that organization to accept a counteroffer. Despite what you may have heard about the brevity of job duration these days, there are still plenty of employers who expect you to stay put. It offends their vanity if you quit and force them into the drudgery of finding someone else. Worse, it's the dead wood that stays put and the star performers who go forth. So, if you're an executive, think twice before you take your boss up on a counteroffer.

CHAPTER 16

Salary Requirements: The Sneaky Ruse Employers Use to Screen You Out

W hat should you do the next time you read a help-wanted ad that closes with the off-putting words "Please enclose salary history" or the still more ominous "Applications without salary history will not be considered"? It's simple. Just ignore those words and reply with your standard resume and cover letter. You're far more likely to have your resume tossed out if you *do* include your salary history than if you don't. The same goes for including a salary range.

Our resume writing service did a phone survey, and we spoke personally with 200 employers who included the above, or similar, wording at the end of their help-wanted ads in the *Wall Street Journal*, the *New York Times*, and the *National Business Employment Weekly*. The results were thoroughly representative of deceitful corporate life, as you are about to see.

94 Percent of Surveyed Employers Said They Consider All Responses

Of the 200 organizations surveyed, 94 percent said they consider *every* cover letter and resume sent to them. Four of the ads threatened *to not consider you* if you failed to provide your salary history. One ad placed by a giant food manufacturer with thousands of employees stated, in bold type and all caps: **RESUMES WITHOUT SALARY HISTORY WILL NOT BE CONSIDERED.** So, did they follow through? They conceded to our surveyors, students at Vassar College, that they sifted through *all* responses. Here's a twist somebody thought was clever: "All responses with current compensation will be acknowledged." Here's to those who fell for that and gave out their salary. Left unsaid is the fact that advertisers *must* look at *all* responses. Ads are costly, and to make the open position seem important and to be certain it will be seen, most large organizations buy much bigger ad space than the exercise requires. So they are hardly likely to miss out on a strong performer by screening people out for the omission of salary. No way. First-class performers—the very type the advertiser seeks—*never* include salary, anyway, and most employers know it. The reason they're changing jobs is often to get a bigger salary. Sadly for the deceitful employers, some star performers just don't reply to ads requesting salary.

Survey of 100 Executives Confirms Findings

We found still more corroboration for our findings when we did a mail survey of members of fourteen branches of the 40 Plus Clubs of America. This non-profit organization helps out-of-work executives over the age of forty to find work. Over 100 members in twelve chapters kindly answered our question-naire. Here's what they told us:

Q: Have you ever responded to an employment ad asking you to "include salary history" and not included it?

   90% YES   10% NO

Q: If you answered yes, did the advertiser ever respond?

   74% YES   24% NO

Our survey shows that 75 percent of the executives who ignored the salary request still got a response. One member wrote, "If goods were sold the way jobs are negotiated, I'd want to know what you paid before I made you an offer."

Owen C., a member of the 40 Plus Club of Colorado, told us, "I know of at least one job I lost out on because I told the employer my last salary early in the hiring process. He felt it was too little at $48,000, and made me unworthy of consideration for his $75,000 job."

Elaine Katz of the 40 Plus Club of Philadelphia said, "Company responded, but no interview resulted because I gave my salary on the phone. I will not be furnishing salary information in the future."

It should be mentioned here that the 40 Plus Clubs' position about giving your salary in advance of the interview is—*don't*. If pressed by an employer to disclose your salary, simply say you won't discuss salary until an offer of employment is on the table.

Disclosure Robs You of Bargaining Power

The right way to think about the salary disclosure issue is to realize that your best chance of getting a substantial pay raise is by taking another job rather than by staying where you are. When a position comes along that you know you are right for, plan your salary discussions in advance to fight off employer shenanigans.

By asking you to submit your salary requirement before you've been given a chance to judge what the job is worth, employers rob you of your bargaining power. It's like sitting down to play a game of cards and knowing in advance which cards your opponent is holding.

Salary is based on two things: what a job is worth, and the availability of people who can do it to the employer's satisfaction. Once a prospective employer describes an open position to you in an interview, and only then, can you sensibly decide what a job carrying those responsibilities and employer expectations ought to pay. By quoting a lowball salary in your cover letter, lower than the employer expected to pay, you may miss a good chance to earn considerably more. I remember a job hunter who found out his predecessor made $10,000 more a year in the same job than he did—$35,000 versus $25,000. (The predecessor had left a pay stub in his desk.) The new employee was indignant at being paid less than his predecessor and took his beef to the man who hired him, who said, "Well, maybe we were paying him too much." I relate this merely to show you how much stretch there is in most salary budgets. Even in the same industry, a similar-sounding position may vary greatly in pay.

Giving Salary History Screens You Out—Not In

Eighty-one percent of the employers we talked with said they asked for salary history to *screen people out*. In fairness to the employer, if your positions were reversed, wouldn't you want to screen out people whom you just could not afford? Others said they wanted to observe a candidate's salary progress to see if they were the type whose only reason for changing jobs was money. Many employers are wary of being used as stepping stones. Still others said they liked to know what a like position paid at a similar organization. That's fine, but let them do their research at someone else's expense.

Be Ready for the Salary-Request Phone Call

Since they can't get it out of you by ruse, the hiring person who likes your resume will attempt to pry it out of you by phone. Be ready for it. (For more on this, refer to Chapter 2, "The Screening Process.")

> *"Hello, Norma (or Norman), this is Mr. Rossi from National Software Products* [the introduction]. *I hope you're as good as your cover letter and resume* [the praise]. *Before we get too far along, can you give me an idea of the salary you're looking for* [the boot]?

If you answer this question, you're costed out mentally. The employer may not have the prospect they thought they had from reading your resume. Suddenly you may seem expensive for the experience you bring. Or employers may regard your salary request as fair for what you bring to the table, but they don't have the money in their budget to pay you that amount. Your caller wants a bargain price as much as you want a premium. Unless, of course, you can get them to think differently. Many people are able to do just that.

One way to get them to think differently about your pay is to assure the interviewer you will earn your cost back doubly or triply. That's a hard argument for an interviewer to ignore if your resume supports you. Wouldn't you rather pay me what I ask and assuredly get it back two or three times over than hire someone less qualified and find you have hired another mouth to feed? Give me the chance to prove it. Thought of in those terms, my premium salary is not a risk but an investment. Think about it.

CHAPTER 17

Cues, Schmooze, and Taboos About Job Interviews: Interviewers Speak Out

I n this chapter, we'll look into our crystal ball and find out what people on the other side of the hiring table are really thinking. The hints, tips, and criticisms on the next few pages come straight from the mouths of employers themselves. The following are their responses to a questionnaire that our resume writing service sent to 500 company presidents, vice presidents, sales and operating managers, and business owners who interview, hire, and fire. Here they reveal what they like, dislike, and violently dislike about people who apply for jobs in their organizations. Each was asked to answer or complete the following:

1. I'm always impressed with a recent college grad when he or she . . .

2. What actions are hopeful signs to the applicant that the interviewer likes them?

3. Does a thank-you note after an interview influence you toward the candidate?

4. Do you ever get anyone else's opinion about someone you contemplate hiring?

5. Do you bring up salary in an interview if you know you're not interested in hiring that person?

6. Is fear of rejection the biggest obstacle to getting the jobs you are qualified for?

7. Are there any other hints, tips, or suggestions you might offer to help improve job hunters' chances of success?

#1: "I'm always impressed with a recent college graduate when he or she..."

As you will see from the responses below, employers want you to know a chocolate chip from a microchip and be enthusiastic about joining *their* organizations.

"Knows about our company, what we do, and what we stand for."—*COO, computer manufacturer*

"Shows enthusiasm for the open position and expresses a willingness to learn."—*V.P. marketing, electronics company*

"Has desire for the job, intelligence, energy, and enthusiasm."—*V.P. human resources, aircraft manufacturer*

"Has had some experience, or at least some familiarity with the field he or she is pursuing."—*V.P. human resources, pharmaceutical manufacturer*

"Has poise and self-confidence and project themselves well."—*Executive recruiter*

"Has good eye contact and is self-assured."—*Chairman, financial company*

"Has had relevant work experience outside the college environment. We are generally unimpressed with recent college grads."—*V.P., large software developer*

"Shows enthusiasm for the job . . . and understands my company's goals and ways of doing business."—*President, cable broadcasting company*

"Can answer my technical questions."—*Software development manager, large software company*

"Emphasizes something he or she accomplished, something that took persistence and hard work in a difficult and competitive environment."—*Manager, federal agency*

"Has demonstrated interest in *us* by researching the company and by asking meaningful questions."—*Operations manager, major airline*

"Has acquired work experience while attending school."—*Designer, womens wear company*

"Has investigated our company and can talk intelligently about the markets in which our company is engaged."—*President, conglomerate*

"Is well presented, knows something about my company, and has a clear understanding of what they want from the job they are seeking."—*Human resources director, multibrand liquor distiller*

"Demonstrates by hobbies and avocations that they have other interests beyond watching TV."—*Chairman, mutual fund company*

"Has demonstrated initiative in some way, e.g., building their own computer, and has real job experience, even part-time, in addition to classroom training."—*President, retail chain*

"Has taken the time to more than superficially research our company and its businesses."—*Field sales manager, large electronics manufacturer*

You may have noticed that the above comments have a distinct similarity to one another. The point is that all employers think alike. If you please one employer, you can probably please them all.

#2: "What actions are hopeful signs to the applicant that the interviewer likes them?"
We asked the employers in our survey whether they agreed or disagreed that the following actions showed a positive attitude toward an applicant. It may help to boost your self-confidence during the interview if you encounter

those actions widely regarded as positive. Just don't let yourself get distracted looking for them.

Signal	Agree	Disagree	Unsure
1. Sets up second interview	88 percent	12 percent	–
2. Brings up salary at the end	55 percent	21 percent	24 percent
3. Asks you for references	65 percent	21 percent	14 percent
4. Extends length of interview	71 percent	12 percent	17 percent
5. Tells you directly	86 percent	14 percent	–
6. Asks you to take tests	31 percent	26 percent	43 percent

"When I am convinced that I've found the right person, I will cease to ask questions and begin to 'sell' the job, company, etc."—*President,* Fortune *500 company*

"I tell the applicant that he or she is a serious contender and then I invite him or her to turn the interview around and ask *me* specific questions about the company."—*Plant manager*

"I am more likely to take a selling position with the candidate and I become a little more agreeable to their demands on benefits and salaries."—*Comptroller, lumber company*

"I have a tendency to start selling the company and the job at that point. A role reversal starts and the prospective employee should then become aggressive with his questions."—*V.P. sales, equipment manufacturer*

"When I feel a candidate is a contender, I begin to focus on selling the job, company, and career opportunities the position provides"—*President, television broadcasting company*

"If I like an applicant, I do not hesitate to say so."—*V.P. human resources, Wall Street*

Negative Signs

There's a message here also for the eliminees, which is this. If your interviewer does not make a fuss over you, extend the interview, set up a second interview, or any of the above gestures, it's a likely sign you haven't impressed them enough. If you're told, "We have more people to see," or "We'll let you know," the interviewer is signaling even more directly that there probably is not going to be a place for you at their company's table.

#3: "Does a thank-you note after the interview influence you toward the applicant?"

The folderol over whether or not to send a thank-you note should be settled by the comments below. As you can see, thank-you notes are a generally positive factor, though not a decisive one.

"A thank-you letter shows conscientiousness and attention to detail." —*Director of sales*

"A follow-up note evidences sincere interest and thoroughness. My mind is made up only to the extent of eliminating candidates who are not worthy of further consideration."—*C.F.O., toy manufacturer*

"Not a strong plus, but a plus. I do not make up my mind until I have interviewed all candidates."—*Manager, export sales*

"No. What matters most is will the candidate make money for our company and will they fit in without creating new problems."—*V.P. Technology, software company*

"Most of the time I have already developed a positive or negative feeling about the applicant, although some require further deliberation."—*Personnel director, wholesaler*

"Personal courtesy is always welcome but this is not a reason for hiring someone."—*Sales manager, new car dealership*

"It reflects well on the applicant as a person but carries little weight in the overall consideration of whether to hire."—*President, drug store chain*

The thank-you note may not get you the job, but sending one will bring you peace of mind that you left no stone unturned.

#4: "Do you ever get anyone else's opinion about someone you contemplate hiring?"

Just look at all the yes answers below. You can bet your life that the interviewer asks someone else for an opinion of you. The more the position pays, the more people the interviewer consults.

"Yes, particularly if the person will interact closely with the candidate in other areas."—*V.P., operations*

"Yes, particularly when the candidate is interviewing for a senior management position."—*CEO, commuter airline*

"Yes, but I don't necessarily follow it."—*Owner, engineering company*

"Yes, obviously more judgment is better."—*Director of manufacturing*

"Yes, it's a company policy."—*V.P.,* Fortune *500 company*

"Yes, never hurts to get an objective opinion from someone a bit removed from the situation."—*President, software company*

We can safely say that the habit of getting second and third opinions before hiring someone is such a standard practice that if you haven't had a second or third interview for a job, the company is very likely not considering you seriously.

Those applicants who seem to possess real merit are invited to a second interview. And possibly a third and fourth interview as well. Why? To prevent you from carrying the interviewer away on a single interview. The most common mistake of nonprofessional interviewers is hiring in their own image. For example, let's say you're a young male executive with a body you've taken care of three days a week in a gym. You interview a young man who also takes care of himself and visits the gym; and before anyone knows, the interview talk has turned from linking your previous job performance to results to fitness and how to maintain it. That leaves less time for job talk and more chances to make a mistake in the hiring process. Of course, the reason your prospective boss digresses is that a) He feels very confident of your abilities and regards you as a contender, or b) He has ruled you out mentally the moment he laid eyes on you and would rather talk about something of mutual interest until he invites you to leave in ten minutes. Thus, a second opinion is a stepping stone to a job offer; you are now officially a contender.

If the interviewer doesn't invite you to a second interview and instead tells you, "We'll let you know," that's probably curtains for this opportunity. Give it your best shot, and if you lose, you lose. There are people they like more; however, there is nothing wrong with your asking the interviewer as you get ready to leave, "I'm trying to improve my interviewing skills; may I ask how you would grade me? Is there a suggestion you can offer?" If you appeal sincerely, an interviewer may offer a tip. Remember, people are flattered when you ask them for advice. Although most may delicately conceal the truth, you have nothing to lose by asking, and you may score some points for assertiveness.

#5: "Do you bring up salary if you know you are not interested in hiring the applicant?"

Here's the right way to look at the topic of salary. Salary talks invariably involve discussion, give-and-take, negotiation, and, sometimes, deception on both sides. Thus, employers won't get involved in all this unless they like you and consider you a contender. That's why it's so important for you *not* to bring up salary first. If they don't bring it up at all, then you know their interest in hiring you is marginal to nonexistent.

"Only if a low salary figure will put off someone I am not considering." —*Editor, consumer magazine*

"I'm put off by a job applicant who brings up pay before he even knows the work involved."—*Operations manager, distribution center*

"Salary is the last item discussed in any job interview."—*President, stationery company*

#6: "Please answer yes or no to this statement: Fear of rejection is the biggest obstacle to getting the jobs you are qualified for."

Just a few words of explanation before you read the managers' responses to the above statement. What was notably astonishing about the responses below is that they *disagreed* with the conclusions presented in Chapter 11. These respondents *do not fear rejection*. They have no fear to overcome. Is Chapter 11 wrong in its conclusion about fear of rejection being the biggest fear of *most* job hunters? Not at all.

The responses of the executives below show that fear of rejection is not a natural fear. It's an acquired one. The respondents below were immunized against fear through their strictly positive attitudes and up-tempo outlook. They *expected* good things to happen. On the other hand, those job seekers who fear rejection have conditioned themselves to expect bad outcomes. That's why respondents' responses to Question #6 above were as follows:

YES   27 percent   NO   73 percent

#7: "How did you handle fear of rejection when you were job hunting?"

As we can see from the response to Question #6 and the responses below, fear of rejection is not a major factor for many of these hiring managers.

"I never went to an interview expecting to be rejected. This attitude is the key you have to convey: You can't afford not to hire me."—*Marketing director, science magazine*

"Told myself it was not that crucial."—*Senior V.P., tractor company*

"You must think positive and go after the job you want."—*President, wholesale company*

"I was too naïve to have fear [of rejection]—the first time."—*Advertising manager, lumber company*

"Was always confident I would get a job offer if it was a two-way fit." —*Buyer, department store*

"I only looked for positions for which I was qualified, which provided confidence and eliminated fear of rejection."—*President, manufacturing company*

"I never thought about the possibility of not getting the position . . . always assume they will offer you the job."—*Manager of planning and development, drug company*

"Rejection for some positions can be good if there is not a fit. Mature people must learn to live and learn—rejection is a reality in business and personal relationships."—*Business owner*

"Being in sales, I don't fear rejection, so I don't see how this would keep me—or anyone in a sales capacity—from getting the job."—*Executive, women's magazine*

"I always adopted the philosophy that I would give the interview my best shot and hope that it was sufficient to get the job. Rejection might be temporarily disappointing, but I've never looked at it as the biggest obstacle to getting a job."—*Quality control manager, pharmaceuticals*

The above quotes reflect a winner's philosophy. If you want to sell your future, make plans now to be an overcomer, not a self-imposed eliminee.

#8: "Are there any other hints, tips, or suggestions you might offer to improve a job seeker's chances of success?"

In response to this question, our survey received a broad array of good advice for job seekers.

"Tell us why you want to work for us . . . do your homework."—*President, variety chain*

"Ask relevant questions and carefully *listen* to the answers. Attempt to find out how you can be a solution to a problem. Give concise examples to amplify an answer."—*Business owner*

"Remember, whether you're hired or not depends partly on you and partly on who else happened to apply."—*Recruiter, technical services company*

"People have to realize that you have to be in the right place at the right time. I have hired people who sent me their resume in the mail unsolicited at a time I needed their specialty. Such applicants effectively short circuit the normal recruitment and selection criteria."—*V.P., software development company*

"Keep knocking on doors and sending out letters with resumes. Usually, we don't need the particular person who has written us, but if we do, it will very likely get them hired with comparatively superficial interviewing."—*Operations manager, beer brewer*

"People usually don't realize that hiring is done by a process of elimination, especially if the employer has advertised a vacancy."—*Industrial relations director, grocery chain*

"Show a track record of accomplishments, not just a list of duties and responsibilities."—*Service manager, appliance company*

"Learn to listen."—*Chairman, bank holding company*

"Learn to speak well. It will get you past the phone interview, and it will help to push you ahead of a technically superior but inarticulate candidate."—*Executive director, trade association*

"Never have a typo in a resume or covering letter."—*Business owner*

"They have to convince me they have a good attitude, not just an interview demeanor."—*Office manager, museum*

"Show an eagerness to work for the company . . . speak up! We get so many applicants who have nothing to say. I'm sure they are nervous, but it doesn't leave a favorable impression. . . . Ask questions. This shows you have interests beyond the paycheck."—*Advertising manager, equipment company*

"Send out lots of resumes. Even if I don't respond to them immediately, that is the first place I look when a job comes open."—*General manager, apparel manufacturing company*

Many of the job-hunting practices described above probably seem like common sense—and they are. However, common sense is (unfortunately) not that common. Job-hunting is stressful. Being out of work and an income is stressful. Stress and desperation often makes job-seekers do stupid things. If you follow the insights above and apply common sense and thoughtfulness to your job search, you'll be ahead of the majority of applicants. And that's the truth!

CHAPTER 18

Changing Careers:
Are You Willing to Make
the Sacrifices?

I f changing careers were as easy as trading in a car, you wouldn't find 70 percent of Americans unhappy with their work. Undoubtedly, many people reading this chapter feel locked into their present jobs. They've drifted into a form of corporate slavery, with golden handcuffs. It pays the bills, but it is toil and drudgery. You'd do almost anything to get out of the job you've grown to hate, but you don't know how to take the first step. Now you will.

As you start to hit your mid-thirties and early forties and your chin starts to lead a double life, you wake up one day and realize that your opportunities to start a new career have narrowed considerably. Even changing from the public/nonprofit sector to the business world, in the identical job, is no easy task because of the surplus of qualified people that already exists for every job opening in the new career you've selected. Realize that it takes only 2 percent of Americans to feed all the rest of us, and only 5 percent to make everything else we need. If the world had a billion more jobs, changing careers would be easier.

There are a number of fears that nag at your prospective employer. Until you provide an acceptable answer for each of them, it will be difficult for you to get hired in a new position. Let's start with an employer's biggest concern.

Question #1: Why are you changing careers?
The employer will want to know this. Perhaps you're starting over because you performed poorly in your past occupation. In that case, the employer will wonder if you'll succeed in the new one.

Still another reason to change careers, employers know, is that you felt bored or unfulfilled, or got laid off in your last position. You're trying to make a fresh start. You want something new that you'll like better. But what happens if you become unhappy in your newly chosen career? No employer wants you searching for your inner bliss on their dime. See you later.

Question #2: Will you perform well and stay put?
The employer doesn't want to waste time and money in training you, only to see you leave after a few months. The expense is not their only concern. The employer probably doesn't want to go through the hiring process all over again after such a short period of time. Additionally, the person who hired you may now look questionable to their superiors for making a bad choice.

Question #3: Can you accept less responsibility?
Chances are you may have to accept an entry-level position in your new career change. Instead of giving the orders, you'll have to take them. Perhaps you'll report to someone much younger and generally less experienced than you are. This may raise tensions between you and your young boss. Young bosses often are uncomfortable giving orders to or criticizing older workers Your new employer doesn't want to deal with an attitude waiting to happen.

Question #4: Are you overqualified?
Will you get bored quickly in this position and either leave the firm or expect a promotion too quickly? Many smaller businesses may not have room to move you up the ladder. The employer may be searching specifically for an employee who can be trained but who doesn't have the ambition or abilities to be promoted. As long as the person can do the job satisfactorily, they want an employee that will be content in the same position for several years.

Question #5: Can you accept a lower salary in your new career?
Can you *afford* a lower salary? You may have been paid well in your previous job and may have developed a lifestyle that you can't afford at an entry-level salary. The employer doesn't want to find out, after six months on the job and thousands spent teaching you things, that you can't accept a lower standard of living.

Moreover, people tie a huge amount of their egos into what they earn. To them, salary reflects their level of intelligence or skill. Most employers realize that even if your budget can take the hit of a smaller paycheck, your ego probably can't.

So What Do You Do Now?

Now that you're aware of the concerns your prospective employer will have, what can you do to get around them? Plenty. Changing careers is tricky, but it's doable if you can show you're ahead of the competition in What-Counts Factors, and you're ten-A-cious.

Get Education and Experience

Going back to school to take some courses or perhaps even getting another degree can help exponentially in launching a new career. Not only will this help build your knowledge of your desired occupation, but it shows the employer that you take this change very seriously and are dedicated to making it work. You may also be able to use the courses to network for positions in your new field.

Second, you can try to get some real experience in your new career before you actually attempt to make the move. Look into volunteer opportunities related to the field or position you are interested in.

Highlight Transferable Skills

You'll want to rewrite your resume *completely* with a definite slant toward your new career. Leave out skills or achievements that aren't needed or wanted in your new career. All they do is magnify the gulf between what you've done and what is wanted. You'll see more examples of how to slant a resume in this chapter's three sample resumes.

Unfortunately, a resume usually works against you in a career change. The reason is it often emphasizes too vividly your *lack* of experience for the new position. It may spotlight ability and achievements that aren't at all applicable to the position you seek. However, you'll still need a resume since most employers won't talk to you without one. A resume accounts for your time, while a cover letter doesn't. Even if your accomplishments up until now aren't related to your newly chosen career, they still show how you excelled in your previous jobs and how you saved money, or made money, for your previous employers.

If you've been a profitable employee for others in the past, your prospective employer will anticipate the same level of success in the future. If you use your cover letter effectively, you can paint a picture of yourself in the new job for the employer. You can explain your motivation for the change, show that you can acquire the skills needed for the new job, and portray how your current skills will help you excel in your new position. These things are not so easily communicated in a resume filled with unrelated past jobs.

To show you how it's done, see the following three career-change resumes that successfully rescued the writers from career oblivion.

Changing Careers: Real Estate Salesperson to Paralegal in Forty-Eight Hours

The writer of the following changing-careers resume got and accepted a job offer for a paralegal position within forty-eight hours of sending out his resume.

It's not always (or often) this easy. Changing careers is a tough problem. But it becomes easier by half *if you bring something to the table that you know the employer wants.* What Martin decided to bring to the table (apart from his degree in paralegal studies) was knowledge of how the government bureaucracy functions and how to penetrate the bureaucratic apparatus to get things done for a client.

This experience was particularly attractive to the lawyers interviewing Martin. That's hardly surprising when you consider that every act of law must be approved and legitimized by the government. "Maybe Martin really can help our firm smooth our dealings with three layers of government," said the hiring person when he reviewed Martin's resume; "it would be a shame if we didn't at least talk with him."

Left out of this resume were measured feats of colossal salesmanship because Martin was no longer applying for sales positions. Other achievements were also left out. Did that hurt him? Not a bit. Employers want short, focused resumes. Also, Martin was attempting to enter the profession of law, where the currency is knowledge, wisdom, and good advice.

Martin also changed his resume to make it more academic in structure. The education section was moved to the top. In a business resume, education would be at the bottom (except for a beginner). Relevant courses were highlighted. The examples he selected showed he worked in settings that required constant interchange with lawyer and client. You might think from this resume that Martin spent all his time in government offices. He did not. The events outlined in his resume took about 20 percent of his time. He just focused on establishing a legal terrain in his resume, and left everything else out.

Note, I classify this as a Mad Brute Resume, even though it lacks the required figures, dollar signs, etc. In the professions, knowledge is the currency rather than profits, and this writer focused intently on his knowledge of law, the chinks in the law, and how to use the law to get a result. If an ant writes a resume and puts a leopard's head on it, the reader will take it for a leopard.

Martin A. Rittner
43 Abbott Road
Hempstead, NY 11623
(516) 555-1234

Paralegal – Entry Level

PROFILE   **Know how to work with government agencies to secure the action business clients require**

EDUCATION   **New York University, Institute of Paralegal Studies,** 2004
                B.A., Liberal Arts, University of New Mexico, 1995
                • Relevant coursework: Real Estate Law, Contracts, Escrow,
                  Land Sales, Fair Housing Laws, Truth in Lending Legislation

EMPLOYMENT
                Development Manager
                Wein-Robb Development Partnership, Perth Amboy, NJ
                (1995–2004)
                Converted single-family residence into multiple-unit office
                building:
                • Put in underground drainage system in compliance with EPA
                  regulations
                • Researched the law and provided the rationale to convince
                  county to waive $3,000 road-access fee
                • Secured permits from five county/local/federal agencies
                • Sold two residential lots to the federal government through the
                  Burton-Santini Act
                • Worked with public officials at all levels, attorneys, architects,
                  engineers

((The Job Hunter's Crystal Ball))

Real Estate Broker
Berkshire Group, Las Cruces, NM (1985–94)
Major accomplishment: Helped expand this two-person broker-
age to a firm of six with quadruple the office space
- Listed and sold residential real estate and raw land: handled
  all phases of negotiations with clients, owners, developers,
  investors, bankers, insurance brokers, attorneys for both sides,
  government agencies
- Completed multiunit transaction involving three properties
  and four parties
- Prepared appraisals, investment analyses, arranged mortgage
  financing
- Codeveloped property from land purchase

Changing Careers: Military to Product Development

The writer of this resume specifically wanted a job in new-product development
with a manufacturer, and he got one about two weeks after mailing this Mad
Brute Resume. Thirty percent of the persons who received his resume arranged
an interview.

Bertram, when he came to our resume writing office, showed that indefin-
able air of achievement along with an extremely agreeable disposition. He's
intelligent and engaging. The challenge was to represent these qualities on
paper. Judge for yourself how well he did it. Bertram's resume demonstrates
how he employed his ingenuity and *foresight* to find new profits.

Notice how Bertram's resume speaks to his reader one-on-one in a conversa-
tional tone, as though he were sitting in the reader's office—rare in resumes, but
effective in this instance. Also notice there are no "I's." The use of first person is
implied. Of course, this resume also has high dosages of persuasion in the form of
at least five of the What-Counts Factors. He shows he understands the demands
of business for profit and knows the role he wants to play to increase sales.

Ordinarily, only a couple of lines would be devoted to military history
when it's unrelated to the work being sought. But on the principle, put in everything that shows how good you are and leave everything else out, Bertram
devoted ten lines of his resume to his military experience.

The reader can insert the "I" in the resume. Please note that you can leave out "I" on a whole resume of achievements, but you can't leave "I" out of a cover letter. A cover letter is written in complete sentences because it is a business letter while a resume uses sentence fragments, where the "I" is understood.

Bertram Wexler
2950 Southern Drive Fort Lee, NJ 20341 (201) 555-1428
New Product Development

EMPLOYMENT
6/01–Present   *Product Manager* (Luggage & Leather Goods)
Frederick Atkins, New York, NY
- Hit a home run with my forecast to management that depressed economy would lead to more 2- to 3-day weekend trips, and fewer trips abroad. *I suggested we focus on duffel bags and built our duffel bag business from $30,000 to $300,000 and rising.*
- Wrote memo to 12 department store chains (480 stores) alerting them to new trend toward "Weekend Gear."
- Placed large orders with several domestic vendors, and several offshore.
- Contributed suggestions to the color palette, offered merchandising suggestions, e.g., contrasting colors, 23-piece sets, *and moved up the price point for more profit.*
- Manage department four months each year when boss is overseas.
- Scan the markets, domestic and overseas, to forecast upcoming trends.

Assistant to Product Manager / Housewares (6/01–5/03)
- **Major accomplishment:** Identified novelty teapot trend / teapot volume jumped from under $15,000 to $1,400,000 / started with a single teapot pattern, built selection to 12.
- Called stores once a week to see what was selling and found my initial order of teapots was a sellout / called six other stores to confirm, then reordered.
- Streamlined product information system: reduced 2-month process to 10 days / new system was introduced throughout our company.

MILITARY   *Telecommunications Specialist E-1,* Fort Gordon, GA
(Reserve duty complete in 2003.)
- Graduated third in class of 45 (Telecommunications Training)
- Trained also in Securities Intelligence in Europe / only 40 soldiers were selected for this training out of 10 divisions totaling 180,000 troops / learned to speak and write German / promoted three times in 14-month period and was youngest Specialist-4 in the brigade.
- Awarded Army Achievement Medal for reorganizing classified document procedures / named Soldier of the Quarter, 1998.

EDUCATION   **New York Institute of Technology,** Westbury, NY, 6/98–3/01
Majored in Electrical Engineering (65 credits) / GPA in major: 3.6

Changing Careers: Customer Service Rep to Training Director

You won't find a more exceptional specimen of a career-changing Mad Brute Resume than this resume of Annie McHugh. It opened doors everywhere, and got her a job in the training department of a major airline.

Annie McHugh
42 E. Mamaroneck Avenue
Valhalla, NY 11041
(914) 555-1234

PROFILE
- Our V.P. of Customer Service got so many complimentary letters about me he asked to meet me.

EMPLOYMENT
6/03–Present   *Senior Customer Service Specialist* (6/03–Present)
Empire Blue Cross / Blue Shield of New York, New York City
Major accomplishment (to date): Had highest ranking (out of 24 specialists) in August
- Handle high-priority problem cases referred by State Superintendent of Insurance, legislators, clients who need okays for experimental drugs or treatments.

- Position requires constant and tactful letter-writing to senators and house members, from scratch, with no boilerplate to guide me.

Special Projects Leader (8/02–5/03)
Major accomplishment: Teamed with one other worker to handle a very large project to shorten response time in responding to claims:
- Retrained 150 processing employees and cut their response time by 1/3.
- Wrote 50-page training manual (they had none).
- Learned newly installed database in two days, then trained 300 others.
- Acted as troubleshooter for workers in any of five areas who were over their heads in work.
- Union 1199 had a backlog of 4,000 unsettled claims / came in early, worked late and on weekends / cleaned up backlog and got current (this achievement was mentioned in my annual review and earned a promotion).

Customer Service Rep (8/00–7/02)
Major accomplishment: graduated at top of my 3-month training class / V.P. of Customer Service got so many favorable letters about me he asked to meet me.

Service Specialist (7/97–6/00)
Blue Cross / Blue Shield of Pennsylvania, Philadelphia, PA
Major accomplishment: Uncovered $573,000 insurance fraud that had gone unnoticed by everyone, including three levels of supervisors who reviewed it.

EDUCATION
B.A., Multinational Corporate Studies, Western Baptist College, Salem, OR 1997

CHAPTER 19

Lying as a Job Search Skill: How Much Truth Is Enough?

L ast year I was invited to participate in a job-search workshop for second-year business school students at the University of Rochester. At a small reception after the workshop, I asked two of the MBA candidates what their reaction was to a survey recently reported in the *Wall Street Journal* that one-third of college students admitted to lying on their resumes. One of the future MBAs shot back, "The other two-thirds were probably lying too."

In writing this book, I surveyed 500 hiring executives (see Chapter 17). One of the questions I asked them was "Can you recall ever telling an interviewer other than the truth about your own salary?" Twenty-two percent said yes; 69 percent said no; and 9 percent declined to answer.

What is one to make of such a response? Nine percent declined to answer. Hmmm. If you add the 9 percent who declined to answer to the 22 percent who answered in the affirmative, you have possibly 30 percent of executives surveyed who felt it was okay to lie about their past salaries. Which brings us to the focus of this chapter.

This chapter deals with a heretofore untouched subject in job hunting, one that is never discussed publicly but is also never forgotten in private. The question is whether or not to lie on your resume or about your salary history in an interview, or whether or not you should make up some fib about why you have been out of work for so long.

Corporations Are No Strangers to Lying

Even great corporations commit shameful acts (remember Enron); however, corporations keep those acts in the dark and parade their virtues. And so they remain great. Job hunters, on the other hand, are expected to expose their shortcomings for all to see, and thus they get eliminated from consideration.

Considering how much dishonesty there is in the corporate world, I pored through all the leading resume and cover-letter-writing guidebooks published within the past ten years to see what they had to say about lying during the job interview process. Not one of those books listed lying in the indexes, much less in the content of the book. It was as though even an index reference to lying might pollute the whole book.

The Standing Advice

The best advice you can follow is to put into your resume everything that makes you look good, and leave out anything that can hurt you. Put in anything you can back up, or anything that does not need to be backed up. For instance, if the company that previously employed you has gone out of business, who's to say the accomplishments you claim to have performed for them are true or untrue? Within reason, you could make up whatever suited the needs of your resume. Moreover, you are *not* obliged to point out your unattractive features in your resume, any more than employers are obliged to point out their own unattractive features in their ads. You can be guilty of the most outrageous occurrences, and none of them need appear in your resume. *Every employer knows and accepts this philosophy.* Employers are realists. They know you are selling yourself for the position, just as they are selling the job to you. A degree of exaggeration or puffery on both sides is to be expected. Besides, for their own safety, employers often run background searches of people they'd like to hire to ensure that they are not hiring anyone who has made grievously false claims on their resume.

What Employers Look For

The following is advice from a large New York City firm that specializes in conducting background searches of prospective employees. Gone are the days when an accomplished liar could invent a whole job history, complete with glorious accomplishments and references from previous bosses, who have all, oddly enough, recently died. Blame it on the relentless march of computerized intelligence gathering.

Employers can find out virtually anything they care to know about you if they're willing to spend the money it takes to hire private investigators. But for the majority of lower-level hires, they rarely do any screening and verification beyond the big four described below.

#1: Drug Tests

Virtually all employers want to know if you use illegal drugs. (Hint: They may spring a drug-use test on you unannounced.) Alcoholics and other addicts cost companies tens of millions in losses through absenteeism, theft, and sloppy work. If you use drugs, better drop them for a minimum of two to six weeks before going for interviews.

We had a customer of our resume service, a recent college graduate, who was about to assume a position with a large Wall Street firm. She said the firm called her the Friday before she was to start, and told her when she reported on Monday she would be required to take a drug test. She panicked because she had smoked marijuana at a party of her classmate's two weeks earlier. She had no choice but to take the test or be turned down for the job. She took it, and luckily for her, passed. But she said she would never have smoked the pot, or she would have arranged her starting date later if she had known employers gave drug tests. When interviewing for a new position, be on your guard for drug tests. *Though laws do vary state to state, your prospective employer is generally on strong legal ground when it comes to testing and does not need to tell you in advance they expect you to take a drug test.*

#2: Driver's Licenses

Have you acquired any speeding tickets? Has your license ever been revoked or suspended? Have you ever been arrested for DWI (driving while intoxicated or under the influence of drugs)? Have you ever been ticketed for inadequate or no insurance? Have you ever spent a night in jail?

Companies who conduct background searches as their main business have national networks of court clerks, in thousands of counties, in every state, who moonlight as public record-checkers on a freelance basis. (Traffic records are open to the public.)

Before you plunge into remorse for past infractions, read on. Background investigators told us that generally, though not always, they check only the state in which you reside. If the offense happened while you were driving in another state on vacation, on business, or as a student, chances are good it will not be picked up in a standard search.

#3: Credit History

Maxed out credit cards may mean you have trouble living within your means. Past-due bills may suggest you can't control your personal financial affairs. A judgment or bankruptcy against you may or may not be a strike against you, depending on the job you seek and the policies of that particular employer.

Your credit history will often show previous employers and may trip you up if you lie about employment dates. If it reveals you lived and worked elsewhere, it may invite further scrutiny of your driver's license and criminal record.

#4: Criminal Records

Any past felonies or misdemeanors, sad to say, can be a knockout factor in finding a new job. Again, it depends on the job you seek, the attitude of your prospective employer, and the nature of your offense. While there are several organizations dedicated to finding jobs for ex-offenders, the shunning of felons by employers is widespread. They fear being sued if present employees are harmed by an ex-felon whose background they were not aware of.

We wrote a resume for a young jeweler with an impeccable, unblemished job history except for one mistake. He was convicted and jailed for possessing $2 million in diamonds that belonged to his employer.

After his release, he sought work only in areas that did not put him in contact with money or temptation in any way. He used the assistance of an organization that helps ex-offenders, and he found a responsible job as an administrator in the nonprofit area. (He did not mention his felony conviction until his face-to-face interview.)

Here are a few more questions we asked the professional background checkers:

Q: Is the polygraph test outlawed in screening job applicants?
A: Yes, in all states.

Q: How prevalent is lying on resumes and application forms?
A: Very.

Q: What is most often lied about?
A: Dates of employment. Discrepancies in employment dates are a very serious issue with employers.

Q: What is your most requested service?
A: Verifying employment dates and salaries.

Q: How do you check dates of employment?
A: We first call the previous employers shown on the resume. If that shows discrepancies, we check things like credit history. Credit card records often show changes in employment.

Q: What percentage of *Fortune* 1,000 companies (the 1,000 biggest companies in the U.S.) employ firms like yours?
A: Probably less than half. Of course, many have human resources departments to perform the services we offer.

Q: Do the giant companies, the *Fortune* 500, employ services like yours to check job applicants?
A: Again, probably about half.

Q: What categories of job applicants are you asked to screen?
A: All categories, from messengers to CEOs.

Q: What resume feature is hardest to screen for?
A: Accomplishments. It's the hardest thing to verify. We have very little luck getting previous employers to talk. Or the boss may have moved on,

and no one else remembers you. The company may have gone out of business. Or the boss may simply nod in approval.

Q: How difficult is it to verify a person's reason for leaving previous jobs?
A: Extremely. Companies are afraid of lawsuits, so they often provide only start and end dates of employment. Small businesses are easier. There you can talk to the owner who feels a greater freedom to discuss past employees.

Q: How can you tell if an applicant was fired for cause if the employer refuses to confirm it?
A: We can't. We can try asking, "Would you rehire the person?" but are often told, "Company policy is not to re-employ people who have left."

Q: How long does it take you to perform a complete search?
A: Three days, except for confirming education. Schools often take weeks or months to respond.

Q: Is a criminal record a knockout factor?
A: Not always, it depends on the job to be performed.

Q: How often do employers ask job finalists for copies of their income tax returns?
A: A few companies do it, but it's not prevalent. It's a legal request.

Q: How deeply do you probe summer jobs reported by college students?
A: Very little, unless the client specifically asks us to.

Q: How effective are the multiple-questions tests given to determine how honest an applicant is? [Developed as a replacement for polygraph testing.]
A: Very effective. [The test consists of a long series of carefully-thought-out, innocent-sounding, often overlapping questions designed to determine an applicant's honesty and to trip up any applicant who lies.]

Q: Why is education not among the four most-requested background checks?
A: It's relatively unimportant after a person is well into their career, except in academia or the professions. Besides, employers can and do get transcripts directly from colleges.

Q: How frequently do applicants lie about education?
A: Frequently, and it is one of the easiest things for an employer to check. You may be in your new job six months before the college finally responds and you are called to account if you lied.

Q: Have you any advice for job hunters about lying?
A: Don't.

Another reference/research-firm executive we interviewed told us that 30 to 50 percent of the background checks his firm performs disclose a "problem," for instance, poor credit history, a criminal conviction, bad driving record, lying about dates of employment, or use of drugs. Facts turned up by these firms often eliminate job finalists without their ever knowing the reason.

A Caveat

We advise moderation in truth telling, not abstinence. You have to learn to be able to sense how far you can go without a lethal backfire that results in firing. That's the whole point of this chapter. There are so many things you might not want to do—like telling the truth on your resume—but do them all the same because it really is the most sensible thing to do.

A Bridge Too Far

Lying on your resume may bring you the long-sought interview, but it also may put difficulties in your way later on, after they hire you. A memorable 2004 case is that of a New York City school official who rose from substitute teacher to principal, to superintendent, to superintendent citywide, to chief of staff, to the school system chancellor with a salary of $152,000. Then, by a fluke, she got caught. Administrators double-checked the references of applicants for a new position they created and found that she had presented falsified documents about earning an MA and a PhD. It took them thirteen years to discover her fraud. The *New York Times* reported the culprit had been "an enthusiastic advocate for the public schools and the city's children." Despite that endorsement, she was placed on an "ineligible" list and will never work for the school system again.

Enter Accomplishments

The biggest hurdle to not telling the truth is the all-points-covered application form you are asked to fill out, sign, and swear to *before* your interview. Expect your interviewer to contrast the facts on the application form with those on the resume, *which you've already sent them*. Exact dates of employment are the first things they check.

One of the things that employers don't check is accomplishments. Why? Because employers *want* to believe what they read in resumes and hear in interviews. If employers distrusted or scoffed at resume accomplishments, then verifying accomplishments would be added to the big-four list. It's just the opposite: Employers incline toward trusting what they read in resumes. Why else would employers invite perfect strangers into their offices based on a resume that came in the mail?

Employers know that most applicants are habitual truth tellers, unless desperate. What keeps most resume writers from lying, of course, is not their morality, but their fear of getting caught.

However, if *performance enhancement* is the game you decide to play with your resume, do it in the accomplishments section. Remember this: *Accomplishments are the part of the resume that are most read, most trusted, and the hardest to verify*. Further, even if checked, you have backup insurance if you follow the policy: *Put in only what you can back up, or don't need to back up*. (Your previous boss is no longer there and no one else remembers you, for instance, or your previous employer has gone out of business, is undergoing bankruptcy proceedings, and so on.) A customer of our service told us his considerate boss said, "Put in anything you want to and give me a copy in case they call me." I hope you get the point.

Only you can decide how you want to approach the subject of honesty in your job search. In short, it's not a smart move to lie on your resume. Job-hunting is stressful enough, so why give yourself the added worry of covering your tracks with a potential employer? That said, subtle embellishment on a resume or salary range is a gray area. As mentioned before, there is a fair amount of puffery that goes on with both sides during an interview. All that I can do is give you some practical knowledge that will prepare you for what lies ahead once you become a real contender for a job, and thus minimize your opportunities to blunder. And, as I said earlier, I know of no job-advice book that does even that.

CHAPTER 20

How to Land a Job No Matter How Little Experience You Have

D on't hold yourself back from applying for good entry-level jobs, internships, or training programs just because you've had little or no on-the-job training. You may find this hard to believe right now, but *you*, just as you are, can still solve many problems that annoy employers, cost them money, and cause them to lose sleep. In order to generate immediate interest in your application letters and face-to-face interviews, you need only demonstrate that you do *not* do some very basic things considered no-no's on the job. The following is a short list of employee bad habits that are guaranteed to drive forty-nine out of fifty employers hair-pulling crazy and make them plead for relief:

1. **Chronic lateness:** Supervisors look weak and ineffective to their on-time employees when they let chronic latecomers get away with it.

2. **Tendency to interrupt others at work:** Idle chit-chat, misuse of internal e-mail (for personal issues, jokes, and so on), and other forms of insensitivity to what others are trying to accomplish together are the biggest single cause of lost productivity in all organizations.

3. **Training difficulties:** Instructions must be repeated over and over.

4. **Tendency to make personal phone calls at work, in or outgoing:** This behavior is high on every supervisor's aggravation index.

5. **Sloppy or inaccurate work:** This important category includes placing files under wrong headings or making errors in columns of figures.

6. **Excessive sick days:** Your supervisor is never certain you'll be there when needed.

7. **Late returns from breaks or lunch:** Supervisors notice when you leave, and they never fail to notice when you come back. That's why they're supervisors.

8. **Objections to any added duty:** A that's-not-my-job attitude forces a supervisor to find someone other than you to perform a task.

9. **Disorganization**: It's not a good sign of competence when an employee can't locate papers, reports, or invoices within that employee's realm of responsibility.

10. **Personality conflicts:** These sap the energy of the conflicted parties and drain productivity. Realize that a boss's toughest job is keeping employees motivated.

11. **Not available for overtime or weekend work:** Overtime is called for when sales are surging or there is some kind of emergency. Supervisors feel you've deserted them when you feel no obligation to stay and pitch in.

12. **A bored attitude toward repetitive work:** Many entry-level jobs involve performing the same task again and again. A bored employee takes long, long minutes to perform any task and makes a caterpillar seem like a speedy animal.

Now, just how should you go about putting this knowledge together to show how good you are?

First, if you have little or no work experience, or if you're just starting out, write a personal application letter, not a resume. A formal resume will just emphasize your lack of actual work experience. The resume is really an employer's tool to screen people out and to greatly cut down the number of applicants the employer has to interview for an open position.

A personal letter is far better suited to dress yourself up as a doer and achiever, as someone who is aware of keeping costs low and profits high, a tireless worker willing to do the jobs your prospective boss hates to do. The letter approach is best if you're a beginner because you don't have to have previous experience to demonstrate how good you intend to be.

A Student Who Continuously Does Wonderful Things

Now put on your running shoes. We're going to run down a list of expressions that will make prospective employers like you more and remember you longer. Use them to answer the routine question every interviewer is bound to ask: "Why are you the best person for this position?" The candidate that promises to fulfill the employer's desires and presents the least risk of disappointment becomes the best person for the job. Here are a few answers aimed at convincing the interviewer that you're that person:

I work until the job is finished.

I'm easy to train; I only need to be told something once.

I'm always ready to do something extra.

I help out wherever I'm needed.

I work well under pressure and never miss a deadline.

I want this job, and I know I can handle it to your complete satisfaction.

Give me a chance to prove myself, and I will make you proud you hired me.

If you give me a job to do, you can be sure it'll get done.

I'm willing to make sacrifices to get results.

I'm prepared to start at the bottom.

I'm good with figures (or learning software, customer service, filing, using the phone, as applicable).

I will never let you down.

When you work these expressions into your application letter and interviews, they can speak volumes to a weary employer looking for a reliable, supportive helper. Realize there is no magic in making two minutes do the work of an hour. It's simply that most workers operate at just 40 to 70 percent of their real energy level because they're bored. All you need to do is exert yourself even a little bit, and you'll find the time to do all sorts of things in addition to your assigned duties. Does this sound good to you? You'll also develop much more confidence in your abilities to earn your cost back, without unnecessary anxiety or uneasiness about how good you are and what you bring to the table.

Think Profitable Thoughts

The number-one goal of every business you approach for a job is to make money. Profit. It's that simple. Nothing is more important to a business person than this word. Interviewers are impressed mightily when a job applicant signals to them they are aware of this top corporate priority. They are still more impressed when an entry-level applicant demonstrates this awareness of the business world, because they don't expect it. Show the employer that you can either save or make them money, and you will have a leg up on your competition.

A Few Words About Pay

Let the interviewer be the first one to bring up the subject of compensation. Talking about money too early in the interview can make the interviewer feel you are more interested in the pay than the job experience. *This is a very typical mistake that beginners make.* Moreover, interviewers may come up with a starting wage higher than you had guessed, after they have gotten to know you a little better. Don't sell yourself short because you are eager to find out how much the position pays.

Finally, if an interviewer does *not* bring up the topic of salary before the end of the interview, it could be a sign of disinterest in you, and you'll want to know that too. Prospective employers form their impressions about you by listening to your answers and feeling you out. If you show enthusiasm for the job, and promise to do more than is expected, they will be much more amenable when the salary negotiations do begin.

CHAPTER 21

The Order of Battle: Six Strong Steps You Can Take to Get a Job

G eneral Ulysses S. Grant, discussed earlier in the book, was one of the winningest generals of modern times. Grant always sat down and carefully worded an order of battle (OOB) the morning of each engagement. The OOB detailed the most urgent goals, the direction, priorities, scheduling, progress reports, and so forth, right down to how each regiment was to be used. Everything was anticipated in advance. Each regiment knew exactly what was required of them to win one battle after another. In a word, Grant believed in preparation.

I've decided to end this book with a personal order of battle for job-seekers that you can follow to a good job.

What Employers Want You to Do

People sometimes lose their jobs because they don't have the needed skills or because they don't know how to do the work. More often, people lose their jobs because they become misfits, out of step with the rest of the work force. Ninety percent of dismissed employees—whether ordinary workers, middle managers, or high executives—were let go for one of these reasons:

1. They missed work on too many days.

2. They regularly did not show up on time.

3. They did not do enough.

4. They could not get along with fellow workers.

Now that we know what all employers do not want, let's run down a list of the six things they *do* want you to do.

#1: Show Enthusiasm for the Job

Nothing is more important.

Keeping present employees alert and productive is one of the never-ending problems of every boss. Bosses have to fight a constant war to get the work out every day. How do you combat boredom in your work force? What every boss is constantly looking to hire is someone who is a self-starter. Someone who won't need the boss's constant motivating. Someone who appears alert and productive, who doesn't have any bad habits, and who is concerned and interested in turning out work.

#2: Show a Liking for the Organization

Prospective employers will love you for it. There are millions of people who just work for organizations but feel no interest or liking at all for where they are. People who like the organization are better workers, have better attendance, are less careless, and create less waste. Learn as much as you can about the organization before the interview, and be the one in five who does.

#3: Use Goals in Your Resume to Show Enthusiasm

Being able to exceed goals is a sign of true enthusiasm. Show your potential employer that you set goals and are capable of achieving them. Before-and-after examples are perfect ways to demonstrate, through specific actions and deeds, how you meet goals. Being number one at something is another. Show how you turned a bad situation around. Show you did a bit extra when those around you were doing no more than was asked of them.

#4: Show You Welcome Change

If you don't change with the times, you become an obstacle, and employers won't hire you. It's human nature to resist change. Most people, deep down, fear change. But change is necessary to move ahead and progress. If you're looking to get hired by a prestige organization, remember that it will surely be an organization undergoing constant change. Show in your resume or cover letter how you changed an old and accustomed way of doing things to a new and more profitable one. It needn't be a monstrous upheaval you caused. Even a minor but important change in work or purchasing habits that saved MONEY will work.

#5: Show You Can Pick Up the Pace of the Work

Your work pace reflects your personality. You can show through your accomplishments that you are a fast-paced worker: faster, faster, ever faster. Employers often feel that the rate of work being done in their organization is too slow, but they almost never worry that it is too fast. Show them that not only can you keep up, but that you can set the pace at a higher level than others.

#6: Learn from Your Mistakes

Laugh off discouragement. Always be willing to try again. Make up your mind that you can come up with fresh ideas as well or better than anyone else. Recognize that the old ways have become less profitable and that change is inevitable to all large organizations.

In Conclusion

Finding a job is time-consuming, stressful, and, at times, demoralizing. Yet nothing beats the feeling you get when an employer calls to tell you, "You're wanted." If you apply the simple guidance in this book, no position you're qualified for is beyond your reach. Now that you know the mind of your employer, the power lies on *your* side of the desk.

Mad Brute Resumes and Cover Letters That Do the Job—and *Get* the Job

A s a sort of measuring stick by which to judge your own job-seeking campaign, read the Mad Brutes and cover letters in this appendix. If your resume and cover letter are as effective as these, then you have clear sailing ahead of you. Notice this characteristic in every Mad Brute Resume: *an instinctive, automatic focus on what the reader wants done for them.*

Resume #1:
Wayne Klein—Associate Buyer

"You're Just the Type We've Been Looking For"

Wayne called us from a pay phone after he came out of an interview with a job offer from a chain of high-fashion apparel shops. He told us excitedly, "They took me to this filing cabinet and showed me a file full of resumes they had received for this position over the past six months. Then they told me I was 'Just what we've been looking for . . . your resume shows enthusiasm, optimism and resourcefulness.'"

This resume is the shortest in the book: 298 words. The subtext (implied message) demonstrates *a willingness to take risks*—a character trait in high demand in retailing.

Wayne Klein
24 Parkhurst Way – 75
Riverdale, NY 23145

EMPLOYMENT

2002–Present **Associate Buyer**—Collections, Better Evening Dresses / St. John Knits
Bonwit Teller, New York, NY
- Buy $16 mil. for three departments, in 16 stores.
- Conceived idea for "Prom Shops" boutiques / 14 of 16 Bonwit stores participated / 5 became showplaces / increased our prom business $1.4 mil./ most stores don't develop their prom business nearly enough, and I capitalized on that.
- Came up with ideas for three exclusive designs that were included in the summer Bonwit catalog / resulted in a complete sell-through and repeated in next catalog.

1999–2002 **Senior Assistant Buyer**—Liz Claiborne Dresses (8/01–9/02)
Saks Fifth Avenue, New York, NY
- Ran Liz Claiborne Petites for one season, buying for 26 stores with sales of $5.6 mil.—up 27%.

Assistant Buyer—Petite Dresses (7/99–8/01)
- Out of school just 13 months, and with the District Merchandising Manager coaching me, managed and bought for $14 mil. department for three months after buyer was fired.
- Asked for and got permission to go $250,000 over budget to invest in evening dresses—increased special-occasion business by 45%.
- **Developed business strategies: Took a hot-selling $200 velvet dress and produced it to retail @ $139 / Sold 600 of the former @ 53% markup, and over 1,000 of the latter @ 50% (also sourced the manufacturer and monitored production).**
- Staked out mothers of teenage daughters as prime customers

EDUCATION **BS, cum laude, Fashion Buying/Merchandising, Fashion Institute of Technology, 1998**
Off-campus activities:
Garden Room Salon was a tiny boutique I founded and operated in Brooklyn Heights (an upscale neighborhood) for 10 months prior to my graduation from FIT / sold accessories and trinkets:
- Arranged for $2,000 opening inventory on consignment.
- Operated boutique at a profit of up to $1,700 a month, all 10 months.

Cover Letter and Resume #2:
Frank A. Fortuna—Toy Store Manager

We Call This a Rezzume

This is one of those resumes that brought a job offer within two weeks of mailing. We later called the writer's home to see how he was doing, and his wife said, "He's working there right now."

The writer, Frank Fortuna, came to our office holding a large newspaper ad and told us, "This job is less than one mile from my home. I know I'm right for them . . . all I need from you is to get me an interview."

The main change we made to his original resume here was to move the relevant toy store material from the end of his resume to a position in his cover letter, where it would be read first. Also, we printed the resume and cover letter on a single sheet of paper, back and front. This resume-and-cover-letter combination was printed on both sides of the page, just as a mezzanine sits between the first and second floors of a theater. So we named it the rezzume.

Has anyone ever asked why a two-page resume needs to be printed on two separate sheets of paper? As far as we could discover, it's because it's always been done that way. Book pages, currency, newspapers, magazines, sales letters, and so on, are always printed both sides of a page. Think of the hundreds of millions of resumes prepared each year. Think of the forests that would not have to be cut down, the manpower, the packaging and shipping—all in all, what a massive saving of resources if resumes were printed on both sides.

Frank Fortuna
395 Victory Boulevard / #291
Staten Island, NY 13214
(718) 555-8897

April 12, 2005

Director of Personnel
Dept. NE 57
Lionel Kiddie City
2951 Grant Avenue
Philadelphia, PA 19114

To those concerned with staffing your new Staten Island store:

The job of managing—or assisting to manage—your new Staten Island store suits me admirably, and vice versa. Let me demonstrate that for you right here and now.

I saw your large display ad in today's *New York Times* seeking a manager and assistant manager for your new Staten Island store. I meet all six of the six requirements in your ad. Lord knows, requirements like these are not rare with me. Staten Island is my home. I've had retail success there managing a large toy department store.

NOTE: The material just below is included in my formal resume. I pulled it from my resume and put it up front in this letter because it's so appropriate.

Store Manager, The Train Set, Staten Island, NY
(The Train Set is a chain of three toy stores all on Staten Island.)
Major achievement: Wholesalers confirm The Train Set was the largest and most profitable seller of toy trains in Staten Island.

- Managed Richmond Ave. store (three levels), supervised two others.
- Took over Richmond Ave. with a volume of $940,000; increased to $2.76 mil. when I left / The two other stores had combined volume of $458,000 when I started, $1.24 mil. when I left.
- Handled store design, windows, interior, and special holiday displays.
- Built custom train layouts for customers / This service grew so popular (and profitable), I hired two assistants to do only this.
- First in S.I. to devote whole floor to train layouts / Central display was 65 feet.

I'm so sure Lionel Kiddie City and I are right for each other, I intend to call you later this week to set an agreeable time for us to meet. Or I may be reached at (718) 555-8897. Thank you.

Sincerely,

Frank Fortuna
395 Victory Boulevard / #291
Staten Island, NY 13214
(718) 555-8897

PROFILE   **Increased same-store sales dramatically in every store I've ever managed**

EMPLOYMENT

1996–Present   *General Manager—Buyer* (9/02–Present)
Fifth Avenue Cards & Gifts, Inc., New York, NY
- Managed 3M s.f. store, staff of seven, sales of $1.2 mil.
- Increased sales from $470 per s.f. to $720 and sales to $2.35 mil.
- Moved card department to back of store / moved gift items up front, giving store a very inviting, decorative look.
- Entrusted to place purchase orders up to $500,000 on own authority.

District Manager (7/98–8/02)
· Supervised five stores, 35 employees, and $11.3 mil. sales
· Staff paid well, trained well, performed well / had sales per s.f. 64% higher than average for greeting-card/giftware industry.

1993–96   *Sales Manager* – Junior Sports Accessories (2/94–10/96)
R. H. Macy Company, New York, NY
Major accomplishment that relates directly to Lionel Kiddie City:
· Helped implement $4.6 mil. renovation at Staten Island store: added 30% more selling space and increased sales volume from $3.2 mil. to $5.8 mil.
· Trained staff of 20.
· Redid fixturing (at no cost) / added a lot of color impact to walls (a trademark with me) / set new merchandising goals / saw increase of 32% in department's sales during time I was there.

Sales Trainee (3/93–2/94)
· Completed Macy's intensive and famous training program / only one applicant in 20 is selected.

1987–93   *Store Manager,* The Train Set, Staten Island, NY
(Please see details in cover letter.)

EDUCATION   B.A., Business Administration, College of Staten Island, NY

Cover Letter and Resume #3:
Forest M. Puckett—Physician's Assistant

Love of the Work Is Always a Safe Resume Theme

The idea in this type of resume is to show your prospective employer that you apply the same energy and enthusiasm to work as most people reserve for recreation. The esteem this writer has for his career as a physician's assistant runs all through his cover letter. He shows he is exceptionally well qualified academically—the first thing readers look for in a professional resume. The second most important thing, of course, is experience. By showing he has a far broader range of experience than the average applicant; Forest demonstrates that he is the best person for the position.

You'll notice a complete absence of the numbers, dollar signs, and percentages that are common in many Mad Brute business resumes. This is because medical professionals are not governed by the same dollar-and-cents, profit-oriented attitudes that dominate business resumes. Instead, Forest offers twenty professional services a cardiologist's physician's assistant needs.

Forest M. Puckett
395 Victory Boulevard / #291
Staten Island, NY 13214
(718) 555-8897

April 13, 2005

Physician's Assistant

Bruce Hayes, MD
269 W. Broadway
Jackson, WY 80076

Dear Dr. Hayes:

I have no ambition to be a physician, but I am only too happy to be a physician's assistant, and to be the very best.

To that end, I have acquired as much medical knowledge as any human can, and expanded my capabilities to the point that doctors have trusted me to do procedures *they* customarily perform.

I have a degree for a two-year course in emergency medicine from Wayne State University (in conjunction with Cleveland General Hospital). This is the longest and toughest course of its kind in the country. In Class No. 9, which is my class, 300 students started, and 126 finished. After completing the course, I took the National Emergency Medical Technician's exam. I placed among the top 10 percent of the thousands who took the test.

In addition to my excellent education, I have diverse experience that cannot be matched by very many other medical assistants. I've worked in two industrial clinics, in an EMS ambulance, and in a cardiologist's office. I love my work, and with me, the patient in need of healing is the inspiration for everything.

My wife and I are moving to Wyoming, and I am seeking a position as doctor's assistant. All of my references are excellent, and I may be reached at (404) 555-1614. Thank you.

Sincerely,

Forest M. Puckett
395 Victory Boulevard / #291
Staten Island, NY 13214
(718) 555-8897

Physician's Assistant

EDUCATION   **A.A.S., Emergency Medicine,** Wayne State University, Detroit, MI, 2002
Basic Cardiac Life Support Instructor's Course, Michigan Heart Assn., 2002

EMPLOYMENT

2000–Present   *Medical Assistant to Bertram J. Newman, MD* (Dr. Newman specializes in cardiology and internal medicine)
- Assist the doctor with examinations and procedures / prepare patients for examination / draw blood and collect urine samples and send to lab for examination.

1997–2000   *Medical Assistant, Michigan Industrial Clinic,* **Dearborn, MI**
- Performed suturing and gave IM injections.
- Cast undisplaced fractures / instructed patients in use of orthopedic devices.

1993–97   *Emergency Room Technician,* **Henry Ford Hospital,** Dearborn, MI
- Performed triage / applied catheters / autoclaved instruments / saw to it that emergency room was always adequately stocked with supplies.

1990–93   *EMS Driver-Attendant,* Detroit, MI
- Transported the sick and injured to hospitals and attended to them en route.
- Treated victims of shootings, stabbings, vehicle, and in-home accidents.
- Delivered three babies.
- Worked 72-hour shifts, with 10–30 calls per shift.
- Taught other ambulance technicians CPR so they could obtain their American Heart Association certification (needed to work on an ambulance).

Resume #4:
Susan Gurvitz—Benefits Administrator

The POW! Right-in-the-Kisser Opening

Your opening is much like a leadoff hitter in major league baseball, whose job is to get on base any way possible and wait for heavier hitters who follow to drive him home. Here's a resume writer who poured such competitive vitality into her first seven lines that she compelled further readership. Including a profit-aiding achievement every two or three lines creates a built-in expectation of profit in those who continue to read. *Note:* This was a two-page resume that was edited to one page here in order to focus on the powerful beginning.

Susan W. Gurvitz
264-15 60th Road
Evanston, IL 32325
(407) 555-2373
Benefits Administrator

EMPLOYMENT

2004–Present   *Vice President Claim Services*
Midwest Claim Services, Evanston, IL
- **First** to develop software for first quotation system by state and zip code for quoting premiums on a national level.
- **First** to provide clients with what-if scenarios and feasibility programs.
- **First** to have a computer-generated product more accurate and more comprehensive than that offered by any of our competitors.
- **First** to introduce marketing program that centers on one-stop service for virtually every function a benefits department needs performed.

General:
- Manage a disciplined staff of 45, including actuaries, claims adjusters, managing underwriters, computer programmers / clients are all *Fortune* 500 firms.
- Design pension plans, stock-option plans, all types of insurance contracts.
- Write all contracts personally / create all brochures, sales letters.

2000–2004   *Vice President Sales,* Mutual Benefits Consultants, Evanston, IL
(Company tailors insurance products to each client's custom needs.)
- Started with zero base and built consulting fees to $2.3 mil.
- Supervised staff of 17 / Performed all cost analyses personally.

1997–2000   *Sales Agent*, Home Life Insurance Co., Hartford, CT
- *Was 30th largest Home Life producer (out of thousands).*
- Exceptionally able cold caller / named member of President's Club.

1993–1997   *Corporate Secretary,* Angelique Terry Health Salons (50 salons), Boston, MA
- First job out of college / began as executive to the company president and rose to above position at age 21.
- Excellent mediator: 30–50 legal cases a year / only one ever went to trial, and we won that one.

Resume #5:
Elmer P. Rogers—Mail Room Operator

Mail-Room Operator Gets Five Interviews from Twenty-Five Resumes Mailed

Office workers are the nation's largest single work group, accounting for half the work force. What do you say on your resume if you are a young man without accomplishments that can be measured in the usual dollars and percentages for a Mad Brute Resume? Answer: You can say all sorts of things guaranteed to breed the reader's confidence in you. And want to at least meet you.

You demonstrate *loyalty* (eight years in the position); *reliability* (always on time, five sick days in eight years); *competence* (by knowing all purchase-order regulations); *accuracy* (found suppliers billing for undelivered supplies); *honesty* (trusted with keys to the mail room, offices, and desks); and *helpfulness* (by helping out with filing, performs personal services for executives).

Conversely, if this resume were written with only buzzwords like "loyal," "reliable," "competent," "accurate," "honest," or "helpful," *and you did not include the supporting information included here,* its readers would consider it to be the usual puffery—writing what others before you have said. Employers want more.

Elmer got five interviews within the first two weeks of mailing his resume to twenty-five corporate office managers.

Elmer P. Rogers
42-24 Yellowstone Blvd. / 4E
Rego Park, NY 11421
(718) 555-2187

Modern Mail Room Operator

PROFILE • Always on time / Five sick days taken in eight years / Work unsupervised / Always available for overtime and Saturday work if needed / Give me a task to do and it gets done / Bank has never been out of blank forms I am in charge of ordering.

EMPLOYMENT
1997–Present *Modern Mail Room Operator,* Swiss Bank Corp., New York, NY
Mail Room:
• Open all incoming mail / route to proper recipients.
• Maintain logs of all incoming and outgoing registered mail, DHL, Fed Ex.
• Fill out all necessary forms rapidly and correctly.
• Use newest Pitney-Bowes postage meters to weigh and post mail.
• Know all U.S. post office requirements and regulations.
Purchasing:
• Order office supplies / Check and compare prices / Order several thousand dollars worth of paper at a time.
• Secure three bids for larger purchases.
• Keep running inventory of supplies, so bank is never out of them.
• Verify and approve invoices for payment / On more than one occasion found suppliers billing for undelivered or unordered supplies.
Work wherever I'm needed:
• Make daily check deposits, pick-ups, and deliveries to other banks.
• Recycle paper to keep trash disposal costs down / Perform office maintenance also to keep costs down / Entrusted with keys to front doors, desks, offices.
• Help out in filing / Retrieve files from off-premises storage when wanted (from among 1,000 file cartons).
• Inspect work of cleaning contractors throughout the bank.
• Perform personal services for executives.

1994-1997 *Shipping Clerk,* Sears, Roebuck & Co., New York Buying Office
• Logged in hundreds of packages daily / Distributed packages correctly through offices on 16 floors / Ran freight elevator, wrote up freight bills and UPS forms.

Resume #6:
Richard B. Davalis—Placement Director

The One Best Way to Get an Employer's Attention

The single best way to get an employer's attention is *to make their problems your problems, and show how you solved these problems profitably.*

The big problem all for-profit business schools face is how to place their graduates in jobs they have trained them for. They worry about it all the time. This placement director placed nearly the whole graduating class.

The big problem that plagues large employers is underrepresentation of minorities in their work forces. It leads to embarrassing court cases, huge fines, and bad publicity that takes years to mend. This is another problem Richard Davalis demonstrates he has overcome. In fact, he considers it his "Major Achievement."

Richard B. Davalis
4010 Hawthorne Street / 14B
Rochester, NY 15372
(518) 555-1130

Placement Director Who Places Almost Everyone

EMPLOYMENT

2002–Present   *Placement Director,* SCC Business & Technical Institute, Rochester, NY
SCC trains a student body of 1,500 for data entry, word processing, electronics.
Major accomplishment: Placed practically the entire graduating class the last two years – a first in the school's history

1998–2002   *Placement Director,* Acme Tech, Rochester, NY
Acme Tech operates 13 schools in nine states teaching electronics, computer programming, and secretarial.
Major accomplishment: Placed 78% of graduates vs. the 35–50% national average for all schools in this category.

1995–98   *Placement Counselor,* Dunhill Personnel Agency, New York, NY
Major accomplishment: Ranked No. 1 among placement counselors in number of placements.
 • Developed a computer desk for agency where previously agency had no placements at all in the computer category / computer placements represented 25% of all placements when I left.
 • Increased agency's list of employers from 40 to 65 through cold calling and referrals.

1992–98   *Personnel Director,* Plaza Hotel, New York, NY
Major accomplishment: Determined that minorities were underrepresented in middle management / looked for promotable minority employees / held regular meetings with white supervisors who were resistant to the change / result: more minority executives / greatly improved employee morale, reduced number of arbitration cases, and enhanced relationship between management and union shop stewards.

1988–92   *Employment Director,* Restaurant Associates, Inc., New York, NY
 • Managed all phases of personnel administration and recruitment for 7,000 employees / recruited for over a dozen of the most prominent restaurants with well over 100 employees each.

Resume #7:
Frankie A. Felton, Jr.—Jet Aircraft Mechanic

Career Change: Military to Civilian

Central to any changing-careers resume is this question: Does this person bring us skills that we can use effectively in our own organization? The answer to that question must always be "Yes."

This whole resume answers that question. It hangs together with a logical sequence—heading, profile, experience, training, and education—that all revolve intensely around maintaining aircraft engines.

A nice touch is the profile, which shows the writer stays right up to speed in latest jet engine technology. Another nice touch is the "Major Achievement": flawless perfection in carrying out the assigned duties in the new position is *the most transferable skill there is.*

Frankie told us that one interviewer remarked, "I wish all our mechanics had the dedication you've shown."

Frankie A. Felton, Jr.
2346 Tilbury Avenue
Pittsburgh, PA 21515
(415) 555-3423

Award Winning Jet Engine & Turboprop
Maintenance Mechanic & Troubleshooter
(with cutting-edge technical training)

PROFILE   • Read technical publications constantly to learn new trouble-shooting procedures for engine systems.

EMPLOYMENT

2000–Present   **Jet Engine Systems Maintenance Technician (2003-Present)**
U.S. Navy, Whidbey Island, WA
Major achievement: Received Salute to Excellence Award for having zero defects in inspection of jet engines I maintained / one of four awarded this distinction in group of over 50 maintenance technicians / also awarded 10 other citations for excellence.

• Maintained jet aircraft engines and related systems, including the induction, cooling fuel, oil, compression, combustion, turbine, airborne gas turbine compressors, and exhaust systems.
• Supervised up to eight maintenance personnel in aircraft turnaround inspections.
• Carried out troubleshooting procedures for the KAGD tanker aircraft and the J52 engines and for the constant speed drive/ starter for these engines.
• Replaced gaskets, packings, and seals in fuel and oil systems; performed fuel- and oil-pressure adjustments.

C-130 Systems Maintenance Technician (turboprop engines)
(2000–2003)
U.S. Navy, Whidbey Island, WA
Major achievement: Received top performance rating of 4.0 for "knowledge, reliability, and initiative" in providing top-quality aircraft in support of Operation Desert Storm and Desert Shield.

• Performed complete maintenance on turboprop engine systems.
• Cleaned and maintained helicopter transmissions, gearboxes, rotor heads, drive shafts, and related parts.

((**182**))

TRAINING	• Naval Air Training Maintenance Group, Whidbey Island, WA
	• SF 31-301/D-704 Aerial Refueling Store School
	• Corrosion Control School
EDUCATION	**Embry-Riddle Aeronautical University,** Navy Campus
	• Certificate in Metalwork (Machining) / Certificate in Mechanical Engineering / Certificate in Physics

Resume #8:
Melinda Mae Dowd—Department-Store Manager

A "Fantastically Successful" Mad Brute Resume Yields Seven Job Offers

We called Melinda Mae a few weeks after she began mailing her resume to department stores, chain stores, and wholesale clubs. "The Brute's been so fantastically successful," she told us, "that my problem now is deciding among the offers."

This resume was so successful because it was so oriented to the expectations of every retailer. Over and over, the writer comes up with sizzling new marketing ideas and fresh revenue streams. She's quick to introduce profit-aiding *changes* in the way things have conventionally been done. She demonstrates she knows how to develop intimacy with customers. Achievements are numerous and *quantified* with numbers, percentages, and dollar signs—the favorite reading of retailers.

Melinda Mae Dowd
49-23 Lenox Avenue / 10E
Manordale, NY 10063
(718) 555-6132

EMPLOYMENT

2001–Present *Department Manager*—Curtains & Drapes / Books & Toys /
Domestics (2003-Present)
Macy's Northeast / Parkchester Store, Bronx, NY (First job after
completing Macy's training program)
- Started with curtains and did so well in boosting sales I was
given all three departments as a reward.
- Built curtain department sales from $612,000 to $920,000 in
one year / found that 6,000 apartments in a nearby complex
had odd-sized windows / ordered goods to fit the odd size and
increased sales 34% / no competing department store carried
these goods.
- Built Books & Toys sales 26% / found trading area was
elderly so I expanded our toys for infants and toddlers as
"Grandparent Gifts Section" / also stocked up on adult games.

Promoted to Credit Promotion Manager: (2001-02)
Major accomplishment: Had biggest increase in new credit
accounts in 10 years
- Increased activation of Macy's card 50%, from 8% to 12%.
- Increased charge card activation from telemarketing from
28% to 43% by splitting the business among four telemarketing firms and promised to give more business to best performer / Previously we gave all work to one firm.
- Promoted card to 100 colleges in Macy's trading areas /
secured thousands of student customers / this was very profitable business for Macy's since most students could not pay off
accounts monthly, they paid 18.9% monthly interest.
- Conceived scratch-off card for employees for every five new
card applications they secured / prizes ranged from $5 to
$100, a very, very popular and effective promotion.

1999–01 *Sales Manager,* Empire State Tours, New York, NY
(Company operates charter buses for sports teams and religious
and social groups.)

Major achievement: Introduced sports teams as a major customer category / we replaced previous bus-charter supplier for 10 teams.

- Cold called on over 100 leading NYC hotels / opened new accounts with Pierre, Marriott, Hilton, Sheraton (half-dozen trips with each to date).
- Developed senior citizen centers into 18% of sales.
- Designed senior tours customized to their needs (wheelchair buses) / called day after trip asking, "How was our service? Could we do anything better?"
- Sold second trip to two out of three customers.
- Developed corporate accounts through cold calling, e.g., Smith-Barney, Liz Claiborne, Federated Department Stores; *Elle* magazine became a major account.

EDUCATION • B.S., Marketing, University of Louisville, Louisville, KY 1999

Resume #9:
Julia M. Sweeney—Office Services Manager

Proving Your Worth after Years on the Job

After twenty-four years of loyal service, the writer of this resume was about to lose her job as office-services manager because her company had been sold and the acquiring company had its own office-services manager. In her fifties, and with a medical history of cancer, Julia feared no other company would hire her.

Julia asked around and found out the name of the person wielding the ax at the company that had acquired her current employer. She called us two weeks after submitting this resume to say she was being retained. Goodness and kindness had nothing to do with it. The sheer volume of the twenty-five duties, tasks, and obligations she was held responsible for either impressed or scared the new management. How can we get along without her? Who can we get to replace her? It might take two people to do her job. Leave well enough alone. We'll get more value from her than she costs. And so Julia was kept on by the compelling logic of her resume.

Julia M. Sweeney
2000 Kennedy Blvd. North / 12G / Boston, MA 21490 / (304) 555-5555
E-mail: jsweeney@email.com

Manager of Office Services
PROFILE   • I have met and straightened out every problem you are ever
likely to meet in a large corporate office.

EMPLOYMENT
1980–Present   *Manager of Office Services*
(Employer's name withheld), Boston, MA
Supervisory
• Supervise staff of 19 for office of 280 employees in 67,500 s.f.
of space.
• Recruit, interview, hire staff for purchasing, telecommunications, secretaries, receptionists, mail/messenger, maintenance,
duplicating.
• Go over assignments with staff personally, explain carefully
what is wanted, so they can make the best use of their time.
• Conduct orientation for new employees, establish office rou-
tines and policies.

Purchasing
• Purchase $300,000 of stationery, forms, printing, and supplies
yearly.
• Purchase over $200,000 of office services (cleaning) and fur-
nishings yearly.
• Buy all capital equipment: two Minolta 450Z / Xerox 1090,
5052, 5046, two Canon laser printers, two Ricohs, seven fax
machines, typewriters, calculators.
• Buy/rent office furniture as circumstances warrant.

Facilities Planning
• Manage all interoffice moves / relocated accounting, computer
systems, merchandising, production, promotion, statistical
departments to new customer service center in Waltham.
• Worked with architect to cut offices, redesign them, partition
open space / have planned and designed over 100 office layouts.
• Arrange for painting, paneling, etc., in renovations.
• Accountable for compliance with OSHA rules, fire and build-
ing regulations, office security, and safety of all employees.
• Handle all repairs, plumbing, heating, electrical.

Administrative
- Maintain schedule of occupancy expense by lease, including verifying increases in real estate taxes, porters' wages, electrical costs.
- Prepare special reports for management, i.e., business given to minority enterprises.
- Approve all invoices and process for payment.
- Coordinate with caterers for Christmas parties, presentations, etc.
- Coordinate travel expenses for entire staff, including rental cars, trains, planes, and hotels.

One Final Thought

Do you want to sell your future? The future is not slow in arriving; it never keeps us waiting. Do you want to continue to burrow along like a mole and be at the mercy of a lack of money, sending out documents that employers refuse to read, and have the whole world of employers indifferent to you? Or do you want to make an entirely fresh start?

Do you want to start having people buy your ideas, bring in a shower of money, and enjoy all the success you deserve until your life is through? Do you want to wear the crown of success, start enjoying traveling, not having to look at price tags, and experiencing diversions of all sorts for your family that are now enjoyed by the successful? It is necessary for you to venture only a little to gain much.

Which brings us back to the very place we started. You have great stored potential and scope for great originality. Almost every job seeker does, if they just knew how to unleash it. Job hunting needs new ideas, creativity, innovation, and a *willingness for applicants to be bold*. The great problem in job hunting is to attract favorable notice, to send out startlingly different documents in front of which obstacles vanish and interviews drop into your lap.

This book explains the demands of the business world for profits, and the role you need to play to increase an employer's productivity. I've explained simply and concisely what works and what doesn't; how to use the telephone in a winning way; the line of conduct you are to adopt with interviewers for a successful outcome; flagging the dangers of projection; what-to-do pointers and clear-cut guidance in composing a sizzling Mad Brute Resume even tough-willed employers cannot ignore.

What I've tried to do is simplify and speed up the process of your finding the job you want and like. I've tried to make the learning shorter, easier, and a lot less painful. All the hard work is already done for you. Every bit of material is right up to date.

I will ask you, after your very great kindness in buying and reading my book, the added favor of letting me hear from you. I can get nothing but pleasure in hearing from you and any questions or observations you care to offer. Everything interests me that concerns you in any way.

Fraternally yours,

Stan Wynett
43-23 Colden Street / 10E
Flushing, NY 11355
E-mail: *stanwynett@rcn.com*

Index

reworking resume for, 139–145
steps for, 139–140
change
creating/exploiting, 89–90
welcoming, 165
classified ads
place of, in job search, 75
responding to, when unqualified, 96–97
clichés, on resumes, 30–31
clothing, for interviews, 53–57
coaching, interview, 113–114
college campus recruiting, electronic screening and, 22
college transcripts, 153
communication
effective, 7
listening skills, 58–59
nonverbal, 58
companies
researching, before interview, 69, 78
what counts to, 87–92
competitiveness, 91
corporate world
dishonesty in, 148
factors that matter in, 87–92
cost-cutting skills, 88–89
counteroffers, 119–120
cover letters, 17, 143
coworkers, willingness to help, 7
credit history, 150, 151
criminal records, 150, 152

D

databases, applicant-tracking, 21–22
dates of employment, 151
desperation, fear and, 99–100
discrimination, employment, 71–73
dishonesty
in corporate world, 148
to potential employers, 147–155
dress codes, for interviews, 53–57
driver's license records, 149–150
Drucker, Peter, 3
drug tests, 149
duties, vs. accomplishments, 25–26

E

education
for career changers, 139
grades, 68–69, 153
importance of, 91
verifying, 153
electronic resume screening, 16–22
employees
bad habits of, 157–158
factors that really count in, 87–92
ideal, 3
reasons for firing of, 163–164
as reflection on boss, 2
relationship between bosses and, 5–6
employers. *See* bosses
employment agencies, 111–114

resumes—*continued*
  duties vs. accomplishments on,
    25–26
  electronic model, 19–20
  electronic screening of, 16–22
  examples of, 167–187
  on file, 18
  functional, 68
  goals in, 164
  humanizing, 33–42
  keywords on, 20–21
  lack of experience and, 158–159
  lying on, 147–155
  Mad Brute Resume, 23–32, 92
  mailing, to reach hidden job
    market, 76–81
  measured accomplishments on,
    23–30
  openings to, 175
  polishing, 23–25
  reach, 18–19, 96–97
  reworking, for career changes,
    139–145, 181–183
  salary histories on, 121–124
  for the self-employed, 32
  sent to HR departments,
    14–16
  verifying information on,
    151–154
risk taking, 167
runners-up, 94

S
salary discussions, during interviews,
  131, 160–161

salary histories
  lying about, 147
  requirement of giving, 121–124
salary negotiations, 47–51
salary questions
  avoiding, 10–11
  during interviews, 44, 45
salary reductions, from career
  changes, 138–139
screening process
  background checks, 148–153
  electronic resume screening,
    16–22
  employers' view of, 14–16
  employment agencies and,
    112–113
  psychological tests, 12
  salary information and,
    121–124
  secretaries role in, 13–14
  telephone screening, 9–14, 124
second interviews, 46–47, 130–131
secretaries, 13–14
self-consciousness, 12
self-employed people, resume
  solutions for, 32
self-talk
  negative, 103–104
  positive, 102–103
sick days, 158
skills
  change, 89–90
  cost-cutting, 88–89
  people-handling, 90, 104
  profit-making, 88
  teamwork, 91–92

About the Author

Stanley Wynett began his writing career as a copywriter for a New York City advertising agency. He currently runs his own resume writing and job counseling service in Flushing, NY. His previous books include *Cover Letters That Will Get You the Job You Want* and *Resumes to the Rescue*. Each has 100 samples of actual cover letters/resumes that brought a flood of job interviews for his clients. His email address is *stanwynett@rcn.com*.